Picture Reference

Elizabethans to Georgians 1558-1837

General Editor **Boswell Taylor**

BROCKHAMPTON PRESS

Acknowledgments

The publisher appreciates the help received from:

Aerofilms Ltd; Ashmolean Museum; Barnaby's Picture Library; the Marquis of Bath;
B. T. Batsford Ltd; Biblioteca Nacional, Madrid; City of Birmingham Museum and Art Gallery;
Birmingham Reference Library; Bodleian Library; Trustees of the British Museum; British Rail,
Western Region; Cambridge University Library; Christ Church College, Oxford; *Country Life*;
Courtauld Institute of Art, University of London; The Dean and Chapter of St Paul's
Cathedral; Devonshire Collection, Chatsworth (three Inigo Jones drawings reproduced by
permission of the Trustees of the Chatsworth Settlement); Dominic Photography;
Drummond Collection, Edinburgh; Essex Record Office; Earl Fitzwilliam; Garrick Club;
Geffrye Museum; Goldsmith's Library, University of London; Henry Grant AIIP; Guildhall
Library; *Hampshire Chronicle*; Terry Hartley Esq; Clerk of the Records, House of Lords;
Sir Gyles Isham, Bart; A. F. Kersting AIIP, FRPS; Leicester Reference Library; Leicester
Museums; Trustees of the London Museum; University of London Library; Louth Grammar
School; Mansell Collection; Geoffrey Martin Esq; Ministry of Public Building and Works;
Museum of English Rural Life, University of Reading; Museum of the History of Science,
Oxford; Museum of Leathercraft; National Galleries of Scotland; National Maritime Museum;
National Portrait Gallery; National Trust; Northampton Museum; Oxford City Council; Parker
Gallery; Hugh Phillips FSA; Mrs N. Philpott; Photo Precision Ltd; Pilkington Glass Museum;
Radio Times Hulton Picture Library; Rothamsted Experimental Station; Royal Academy of Arts;
Royal Commission on Historical Documents; Royal Ontario Museum, University of Toronto;
Lord Salisbury; School of Scottish Studies, University of Edinburgh; Science Museum (for
Crown copyright photographs); B. A. Seaby Ltd; Alfred H. Smith Esq; University of Reading;
Tate Gallery; Trustees of the Tichborne Estate; P. E. Towler Esq; Valentine & Sons Ltd;
Victoria and Albert Museum (for Crown copyright photographs); Rex Wailes Esq; The Warden
and Fellows of All Souls College, Oxford; Josiah Wedgwood & Sons Ltd; The Wellcome
Institute of the History of Medicine; Welsh Folk Museum, Cardiff; Royal Library, Windsor
Castle; Woodbridge Church, Suffolk; Worshipful Company of Glovers

ISBN 0 340 14908 6

First printed in this form 1971
Published by Brockhampton Press Ltd, Salisbury Road, Leicester
Printed in Great Britain by Jarrold & Sons Ltd, Norwich
Text copyright © 1965, 1969, 1970, 1971 Boswell Taylor
Illustrations copyright © 1965, 1969, 1970 Brockhampton Press Ltd

Contents

Events in British history, 1558 to 1837

1558 Elizabeth acceded to the English throne.
1568 Mary Queen of Scots fled to England.
1571 Thirty-nine Articles of Faith (constitution of the Church of England) sanctioned by Convocation.
1585 Elizabeth at war with Spain.
Earl of Leicester led troops to help Dutch against Spain.
1586 Babington Plot (to free Mary and kill Elizabeth) revealed.
1587 Mary Queen of Scots executed.
Drake raided Cadiz: damage to fleet delayed Spanish Armada.
1588 Defeat of Spanish Armada.
1592 Presbyterian system of government established in Scotland.
1599 Earl of Essex banished after failing to crush Irish Rebellion.
James VI of Scotland asserted Divine Right of Kings.
1600 Lord Mountjoy began subjugation of Ireland.
1601 Failure of Essex insurrection led to his execution.
1603 Accession of James VI of Scotland as James I of England.
1605 Gunpowder Plot to blow up Houses of Parliament discovered.
1625 Accession of Charles I.
1628 Parliament passed Petition of Right claiming the legal freedoms and declaring certain acts of Charles to be unconstitutional.
1638 Scottish National Covenant drawn up to defend their religion.
1639 Charles I levied troops against Scottish Covenanters.
1641 Thomas Wentworth, Earl of Stafford, tried and executed.
Outbreak of rebellion in Ireland.
1642 Charles I failed to arrest five rebellious MPs.
Outbreak of Civil War.
1643 Solemn League and Covenant: agreement between Scots and Parliament.
1644 Cromwell defeated Charles at Marston Moor: decisive battle of the Civil War.
1646 Surrender of Charles I to the Scots at Newark.
1647 Charles surrendered to Parliament.
1648 Scots defeated by Cromwell at Preston.
1649 Trial and execution of Charles I.
Proclamation of England as Commonwealth.
Cromwell suppressed Irish rebellion.
1651 Cromwell defeated the future Charles II at Worcester.
1653 Cromwell appointed Lord Protector.
1660 Charles II restored to the English throne.
1666 Great Fire of London followed Great Plague (1665).
1672 Second Declaration of Indulgence followed by Test Act (1673).
1685 Accession of James II to English throne.
Duke of Monmouth defeated at Sedgemoor.
1688 Glorious Revolution; James II fled; William of Orange landed in Torbay.
1689 Declaration of Rights; William III and Mary II proclaimed king and queen.
James II defeated at Battle of the Boyne.
1701 Act of Settlement established Protestant succession.
1702 War of Spanish Succession: result of Louis XIV's intrigues.
William III died.

1702 Queen Anne succeeded to the throne.
1704 Marlborough won victory at Blenheim.
1707 Act of Union united Scottish and English Parliaments.
1713 Treaty of Utrecht ended War of Spanish Succession.
1714 Accession of George I, Elector of Hanover.
1715 Jacobites defeated at Preston.
1720 'South Sea Bubble' burst following share-buying mania.
Government took over National Debt.
Walpole appointed Chancellor of the Exchequer and First Lord of Treasury (Prime Minister).
1727 Accession of George II.
1730 John and Charles Wesley formed Methodist Society.
1739 War of Jenkins' Ear; war with Spain.
1744 War of the Austrian Succession; formal declaration of war on Britain and Austria by France.
1745 Battle of Dettingen; British and Hanoverian army led by George II defeated French.
Jacobite Rebellion in Scotland and England led by Prince Charles Edward ('Bonnie Prince Charlie').
1746 Jacobites defeated by Duke of Cumberland at Culloden Moor.
1748 Treaty of Aix-la-Chapelle ended War of the Austrian Succession.
1754 Outbreak of hostilities between Britain and France in North America.
1756 Outbreak of Seven Years War; France and Austria (Russia later) against Britain and Prussia.
1757 Clive won Battle of Plassey in India.
1759 Wolfe captured Quebec from the French.
1760 Accession of George III, grandson of George II.
1763 Treaty of Paris ended Seven Years War.
1775 American War of Independence: Declaration of Independence issued by North American colonists.
1783 Treaty of Versailles ended American War of Independence.
1798 Irish Rebellion led by Wolfe Tone and Emmet suppressed.
1800 Act of Union with Ireland united Parliament of Britain and Ireland.
1805 Battle of Trafalgar: French and Spanish fleets defeated by Nelson.
Nelson killed in the battle.
1811 Prince of Wales became Regent.
1815 Napoleon exiled to Elba.
Battle of Waterloo: Napoleon defeated by Wellington and Blücher.
1816 Napoleon banished to St Helena.
1820 Accession of Prince Regent as George IV.
1828 Wellington became Prime Minister.
1830 Accession of Duke of Clarence as William IV.
1832 Parliamentary Reform Act passed.
1833 Abolition of Slavery Act passed.
1834 Tolpuddle Martyrs: attempt to set up farm labourers' union failed.
Grand National Consolidated Trades Union of Great Britain and Ireland set up by Robert Owen.
1837 Accession of Queen Victoria.

Elizabethans

Consultant Historian: John West, MA
Illustrator: Leslie Marshall, MSIA

THE ELIZABETHAN PERIOD is regarded as the Golden Age in British history. Queen Elizabeth, who was known with affection as the 'Virgin Queen', 'Gloriana' and 'Good Queen Bess', ruled for 45 years, from 1558 to 1603. With pride and cunning she defied the might of Spain, and her little ships battled against the proud Armada and sent the broken remnants of the great fleet scurrying back to Spain. Sailors such as Frobisher and Hawkins went adventuring on the high sea, and Francis Drake's Golden Hind *was the first British ship to sail round the world. At home poets like Edmund Spenser and Walter Raleigh wrote some of the finest poems in the English language. Christopher Marlowe's plays are still read and acted. And it was during these golden years that many of Shakespeare's plays were written.*

Dice-box

Jousting

Sports and Pastimes

Children's games

Part of the border of the Bradford Table Carpet

Boar hunting

Wooden doll

Hobby-horse

Hunting

The Elizabethans made their own amusements. At court during the long winter evenings there was dancing, music and revels. Young people played such games as blind-man's-buff and shuttlecock. From the rushlit corners came the click of chess-men and the rattle of dice. In summer, people liked to enjoy themselves out of doors, in cobbled streets or on the village green.

6

Nine pin bowling

Circular chess-board

Table bowls

Crossbow

Longbow

Fowling

Hawking

For the rich people there was the pageantry of jousting and the thrill of hunting and hawking. Other folk wrestled and danced and played games where they could. The football they played had no rules, and the only goal was to get the ball into their own parish. And always there was archery— enforced by law; a pastime that could bring death to the foes of England.

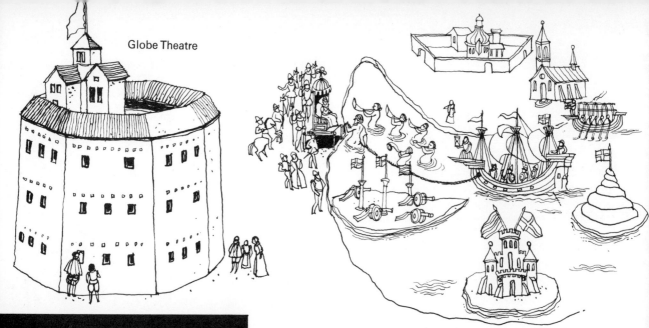

Globe Theatre

The Queen attends a water masque

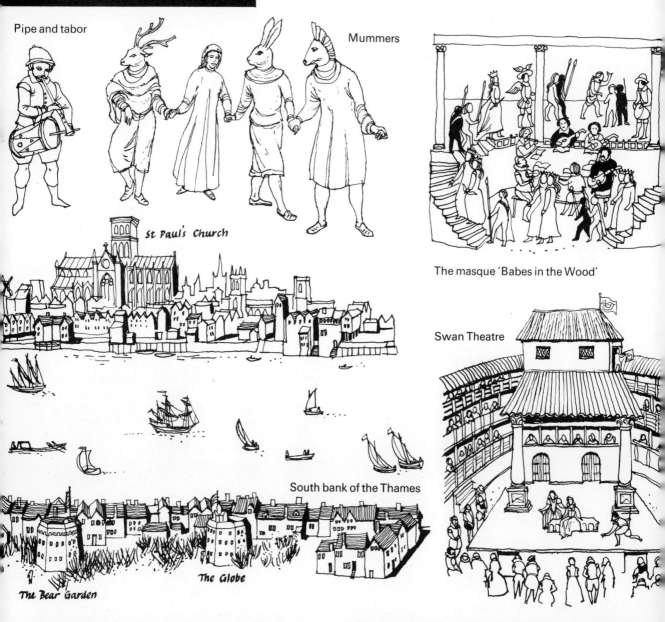

Pipe and tabor

Mummers

St Paul's Church

The masque 'Babes in the Wood'

Swan Theatre

South bank of the Thames

The Bear Garden

The Globe

This was the age of Shakespeare and Marlowe. Companies of players toured the countryside, and acted their plays in inn-yards, wherever they could find an audience. But the heart of drama was in the little open-air theatres on the banks of the River Thames. Here, too, were the water masques, and for blood-thirsty citizens, the bear-baiting and bull-rings.

8

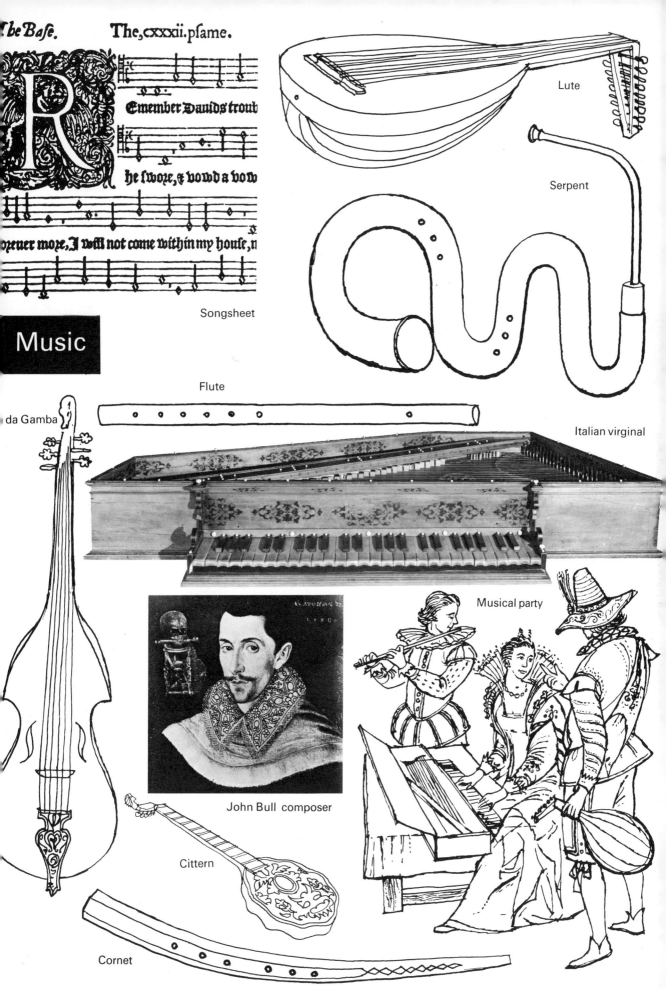

The Base. The,cxxxii.pfame.

Remember Dauids troub

he fwore, & vowd a vow

euer moze, I will not come within my house, n

Songsheet

Music

Lute

Serpent

Flute

da Gamba

Italian virginal

John Bull composer

Musical party

Cittern

Cornet

The Elizabethans lived with music. Lutes were as much a part of the homes as pewter jugs and silver plates. Courtiers composed songs to the ladies they loved. A musical evening was a common event tor burghers and their wives. Peasants plucked reeds from the river bank and made their own pipes. A popular form of song was the madrigal, with several voices singing separate melodies.

Seal of Louth Grammar-School

Stratford-upon-Avon
Grammar-School

Schools

Hornbook with the alphabet and
other lessons that had to be learnt

Quill

ORATIONI, O VERO ME
ditationi dalle quali la mente
è incitata a patientemente pa
tire ogni afflittione, et sprezzare
la vana prosperita di questo mō
do, et sempre desiderare l'eterna
beatitudine: raccolte da alcune
sante opere, per la valorosissima,
et humanissima princessa, Cathe
rina reina d'inghilterra, francia
et hibernia. Tradotte per la signo
ra Elizabetta dalla lingua inglese
in vulgare italiano.

Prayers in the handwriting of Princess Elizabe[th]

Few children were lucky enough to go to school.
Even Shakespeare's father, who was an alderman,
could not write his own name. Latin and Greek
10 were the main subjects in the grammar schools.

The swish of the birch was commonly heard.
Tutors taught the daughters of wealthy families.
Princess Elizabeth was taught by one of the most
famous schoolmasters of all—Roger Ascham.

Gold angel

Watchman

Handloom weaving

Hammered sixpences

Silver half-crown

Townspeople at Work

Hammered shilling

Fire fighting

Groat

Milled sixpence

Sculptor

Painter

Printing

Typesetting

In the stocks

Milled sixpence

Bookbinding

Carpenters

Water carrier

Surgical instruments

The towns were small, without factories or mills. Men worked in their own homes, in sheds, or in the open. Printers and bakers, and men in similar trades that needed heavy machinery, worked together in large rooms, which were often part of the master's home. Women had their own spinning-wheels, but most of the weavers were men who worked for long hours in their own cottages.

11

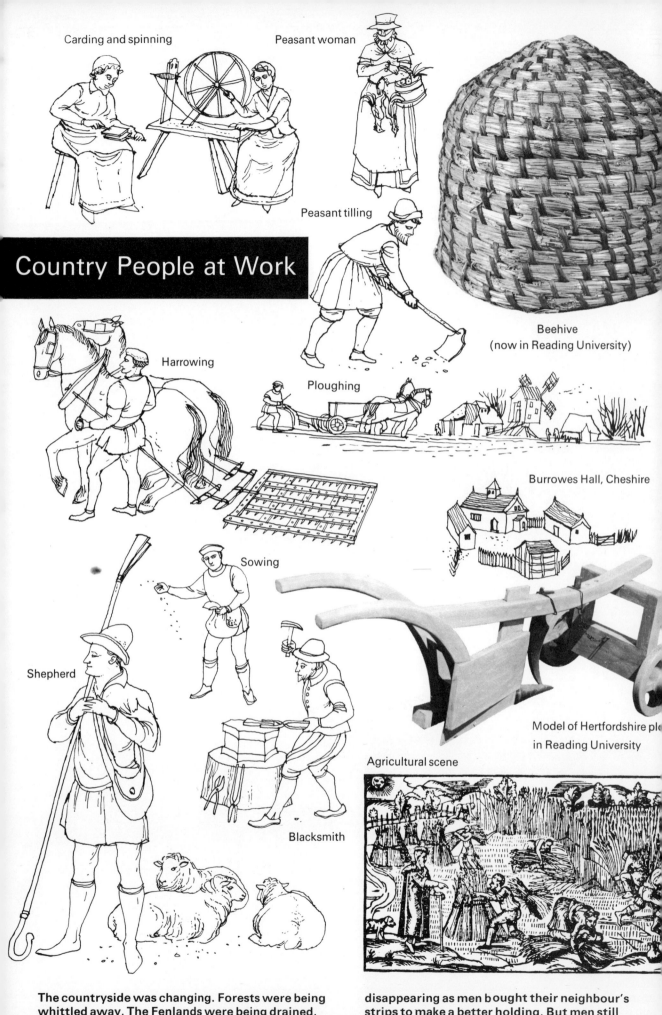

Carding and spinning

Peasant woman

Peasant tilling

Beehive
(now in Reading University)

Country People at Work

Harrowing

Ploughing

Burrowes Hall, Cheshire

Sowing

Shepherd

Blacksmith

Model of Hertfordshire plo
in Reading University

Agricultural scene

The countryside was changing. Forests were being whittled away. The Fenlands were being drained. Landowners enclosed common land and grew rich from the sale of wool. Strip farming was gradually

disappearing as men bought their neighbour's strips to make a better holding. But men still challenged nature with primitive implements to win a living from the soil.

Markets and Shops

Shops

Barber's shop

Shop signs

Bellman

Water carriers

Tradesmen's token

Fishmonger's

Lantern

Poorbox

Salter's

Watchman

Eastcheap Market

Pillory

Along the narrow streets with their open shops and overhanging bedrooms bustled the country folk on market day. This was more than a time for selling a pig or buying a hen. This was the time to meet neighbours, to make the purchases of the week, and to strike a bargain. Now news was exchanged and men shared gossip in the ale-house before setting off home.

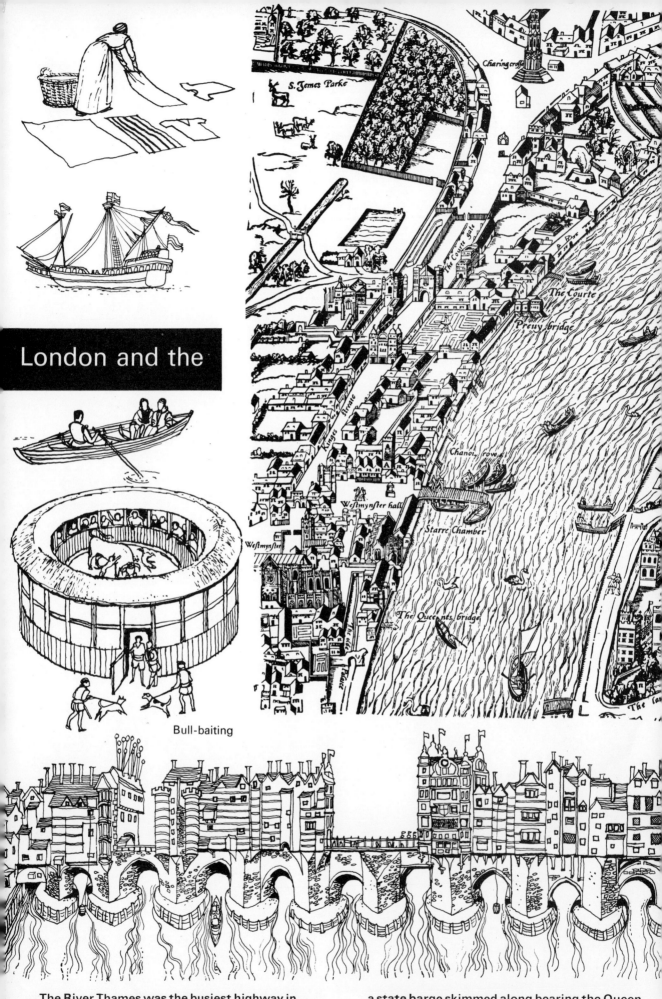

London and the

Bull-baiting

Charing crosse

S. Iemes Parke

The Courte Gate

The Courte

Preuy bridge

Kinges Streate

Chanon row

Westmynster hall

Starre Chamber

Westmynster

The Queenes bridge

The River Thames was the busiest highway in London. On its waters, which rose and ebbed with the tide, went skiffs and barges. Apprentices were proud of their skill with an oar. Sometimes a state barge skimmed along bearing the Queen, or perhaps a traitor on his way to the Tower. London Bridge was like a little village with houses and shops over its many arches. Stuck on

14

wre hyll

Poſtern gate

The Towre
of London

Wharf at low tide

the water worke

poles above the roof tops were the heads of traitors as a warning to anyone who contemplated treason. And on the tide, with sails filling with the wind, went the little galleons upon their voyages to the other side of the world. Women used the grassy banks to lay out washing. On the river banks, too, were the theatres and bull-baiting arenas. The river was a part of London life.

15

Royal coach

The Feathers Inn, Ludlow

Travelling by Road

Riding pillion

Litter

Travelling shoemaker

Doeskin saddle

Tavern dining-roo

The Queen arrives at Nonesuch Palace

By law, every common labourer of town and country had to work for six days in the year upon the roads in his district. The highways received no other attention. As villagers rarely welcomed

visitors they did not do their road work duties with much enthusiasm. In winter roads were muddy and rutted. They were thick with dust in summer. No one travelled unless he had to, and then he

avelling trunk

er bottle

The Queen in progress in her state litter

Country revellers round a coach

Wealthy traveller in his touring carriage

State coach

armer's wife returns from market

Pack-horse

tried to join companions for protection against highway robbers. Sometimes pedlars, priests or vagrants went bravely on their own. But most travellers went in groups. A troop of soldiers sometimes passed. And in the spring, when smells and fevers came to the town, rich people travelled magnificently in coaches to their country homes.

Ships

Sir John Hawkins, merchant adventurer

The ship that carried Sir Philip Sidney's body to England

Shipmaker marks out the plan before transferring the drawing to the floor of the moulding loft

Shipwright selects wood from suitable trees

Midship section of a new ship

Drake's badge

Sir Francis Drake

Merchant ship

With pennants flying and drums sounding, the little wooden ships set sail from English ports for the rich lands beyond the seas. They set out bravely, but they gambled with death.

They did not know enough about diets to keep well on long voyages. The crews were half-starved and rotten with scurvy. The ships' instruments to set a course were crude and often

18

The Seal of Southampton

Howard of Effingham, Lord Admiral of England and Commander-in-Chief of the English fleet which defeated the Armada

Ark Royal, Howard's flagship

faulty. The sailors had to use their wits, strength and seamanship to ride through storms. A distant sail could mean an enemy. There were no lighthouses to warn them of danger, or charts to show hidden rocks. And yet the sailors on the Elizabethan ships charted the seas, discovered new lands, and lay claim to distant lands. They established England's sea power for centuries.

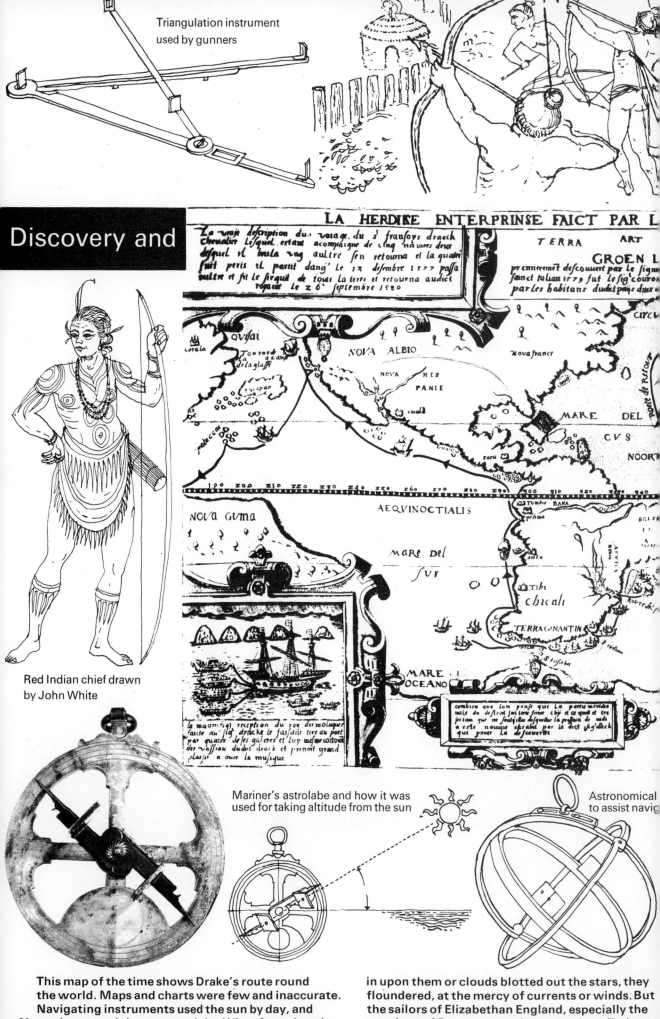

Triangulation instrument used by gunners

LA HERDIKE ENTERPRINSE FAICT PAR L...

Red Indian chief drawn by John White

Mariner's astrolabe and how it was used for taking altitude from the sun

Astronomical ... to assist navig...

This map of the time shows Drake's route round the world. Maps and charts were few and inaccurate. Navigating instruments used the sun by day, and mariners used the stars at night. When fogs closed in upon them or clouds blotted out the stars, they floundered, at the mercy of currents or winds. But the sailors of Elizabethan England, especially the sea-dogs of Devon, were always ready to find out

Red Indians attacking a fort by John White, one of the original settlers

Drake's Dial, and aid to navigation combining compass, quadrant, latitude and tide tables

Quadrant

Invention

R DRAECK D'AVOIR CIRQVIT TOVTE LA TERRE

Sailor using quadrant

Red Indian chief's wife and child drawn by John White

Astronomical compendium containing instruments to help navigation

Rocket

more about unplotted seas and unmapped lands. They sought new ways to the spice lands. They were prepared to fight the great Spanish galleons to win their share of the treasures of the New World. Then they returned with their own tales of the wonderful things they had seen. John White was one of these travellers and his drawings of Red Indians are true.

The Armada

Weapons and armour

Victory medal

Griffin (British)

King Philip II of Spain

Spanish galleass

Don Hugo de Moncada (Spanish squadron leader)

Beacon

White Bear (British)

Victory m

Spaniards called Drake the Devil. They grew more impatient at the attacks upon their ships. King Philip II of Spain finally decided to build a great fleet of ships. This Armada would carry his army and land it upon the shores of England. On the 19th July, 1588 the great Spanish Armada, in crescent form, came within sight of the country it meant to conquer. The beacons gave the alarm as

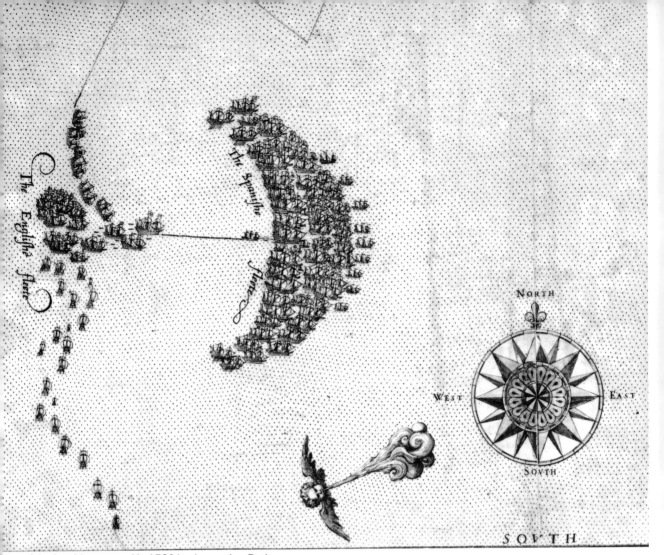

Plan of the battle, engraved in 1590 by Augustine Ryther

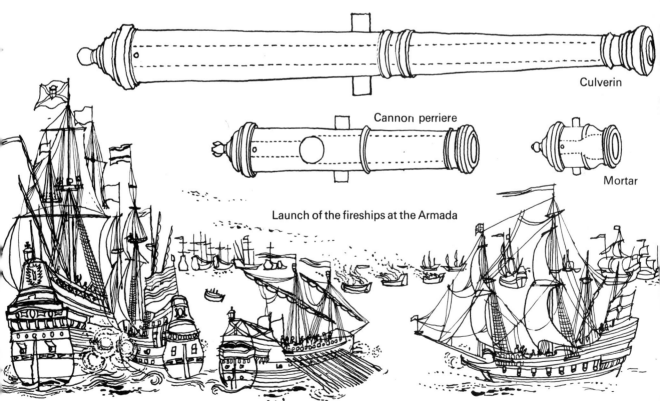

Culverin

Cannon perriere

Mortar

Launch of the fireships at the Armada

they leapt into flame along the coast, and sent the message from hill to hill. Soldiers gathered at Tilbury. They cheered the Queen when she visited them, and said that they would never give in. But they were never called upon. Fire-ships worried the ships in Calais harbour. Then, after the battle, the storm broke. It was the end of the proud Armada. The remnants made their battered way home.

23

Long-bowman and pikeman

Matchlock arquebus

Armoured car

Armour made for the Earl of Cumberland

Plate armour

Cannon

Loading cannon

Cavalry pistol

Morion

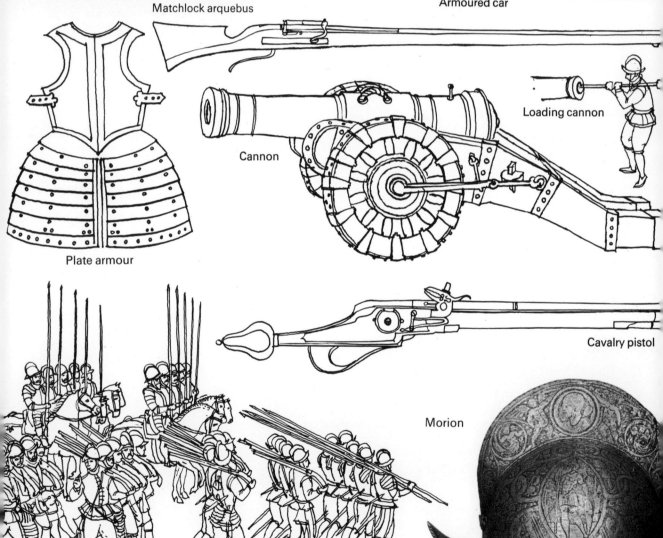
English army on the march

Gunpowder had been invented. Heavy cannon balls were put in the cannon's mouth. Powder was rammed home. A spark, a flash, a roar, and the cannon ball sped on its way, to smash down gates and walls, and to make a way for the soldiers. Bows and arrows were still used, and men fought in combat hand to hand. They wore breastplates and helmets, and some wore heavy armour.

24

Mary, Queen of Scots

Lady

Royal hunting picnic

Queen Elizabeth's fan

Man's cap

Young man

Sir Christopher Hatton

Sir Philip Sidney

London merchant and his wife

This was the time of ruffs and farthingales, bejewelled head-dresses and shaped stomachers. Men were as gaily dressed as the ladies. They had magnificently lined cloaks. Their doublet and hose were gaily coloured. Embroidery was an art, and clothes were worn more for ornament than comfort. In the ballroom they were beautiful, but not fitting for country wear, even on a picnic.

25

Town women with a country woman

Cowherd

Dress

Sheriff

English cottager's wife (Holbein)

Lady of the Manor   Commoner

Vagabond and a beggar

Country folk dancing to music
played on the bagpipes

Archer and a
commoner

Children dressed
like adults

Away from court people dressed more soberly,
but men still liked to wear slashed doublets.
Women wore bulky clothing, which must have
26 been warm in winter, but very hot in summer.

Most of the cloth for clothes was woven in
villagers' own homes. It was homespun and
rough, dyed with flower and leaf juice from the
hedgerows. Men made their own leather shoes.

Buff tunic with leather facing and silk ribbon 'points'

Man's leather hat slashed to show the silk lining

Spanish farthingale beneath dress

Lord of the Manor

Hat jewel

Man's leather gauntlets with silk-lined cuffs

Woman's silk bodice

Sir Edward Hoby

Coif (hood)

Iron corset probably for deformed figure

Fitting the farthingale

The Elizabethan courtiers and their wives took delight in their possessions. They were fond of jewellery, which men as well as women wore. Buckles and hatpins were bejewelled.

Women admired small waists and were prepared to wear tight iron corsets. Hooped petticoats called farthingales were worn to swell out embroidered skirts. The dangling purse, or reticule, held keys.

Hardwick Hall

Mansions and Houses

Courtyard gates   Holdenbury, Northamptonshire

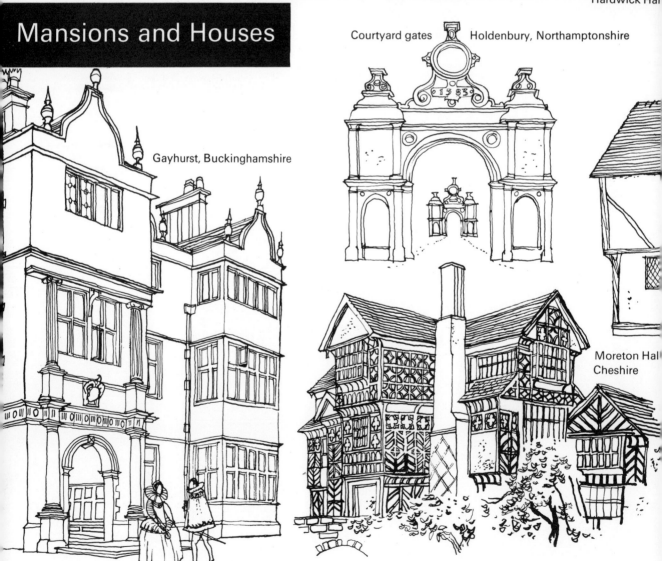

Gayhurst, Buckinghamshire

Moreton Hall
Cheshire

During the reign of the Tudors men began to feel more secure. They no longer needed to live in castles and fortresses. They began to build
28 beautiful mansions and houses, with plenty of

glass windows. Many of them were built to an E plan, some said out of compliment to the Queen. Overhanging bedrooms gave more strength to the buildings. Splendid wooden staircases opened from

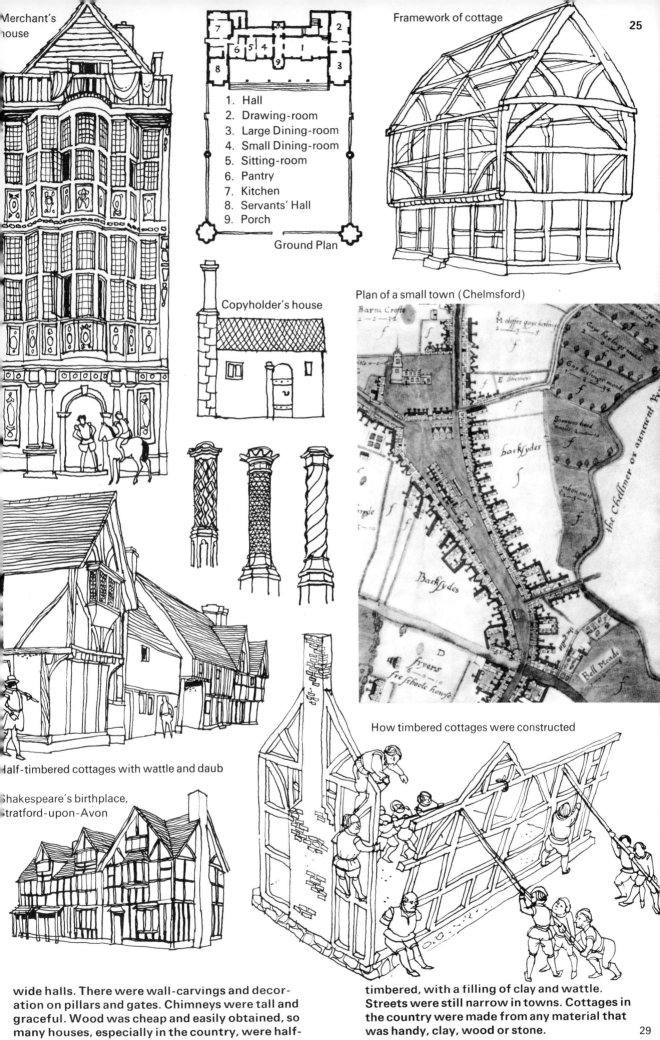

Merchant's house

Framework of cottage

Ground Plan

1. Hall
2. Drawing-room
3. Large Dining-room
4. Small Dining-room
5. Sitting-room
6. Pantry
7. Kitchen
8. Servants' Hall
9. Porch

Copyholder's house

Plan of a small town (Chelmsford)

How timbered cottages were constructed

Half-timbered cottages with wattle and daub

Shakespeare's birthplace, Stratford-upon-Avon

wide halls. There were wall-carvings and decoration on pillars and gates. Chimneys were tall and graceful. Wood was cheap and easily obtained, so many houses, especially in the country, were half-

timbered, with a filling of clay and wattle. Streets were still narrow in towns. Cottages in the country were made from any material that was handy, clay, wood or stone.

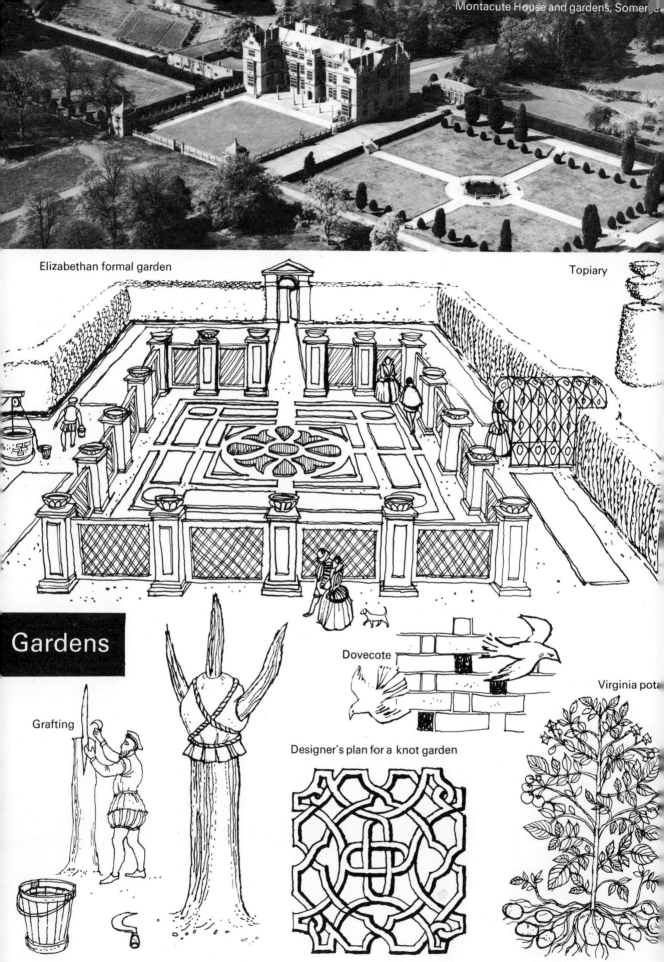

Elizabethan formal garden

Topiary

Gardens

Grafting

Dovecote

Virginia pota

Designer's plan for a knot garden

Herbs for the still-room, sweet-perfumed flowers to be crushed to make scent, rose petals in the pot-pourri bowl, fruit for the meal—all these were grown in the trim gardens of manor houses.

Gardens were laid out formally, with paths and hedges. Lawns were laid and close cut. Fruit grafting was practised. There were sundials and dovecotes. During winter the doves were eaten.

Wrought-iron basket spit

Earthenware dish

Dairy

Upright toaster with plate carrier

Kitchens

Preparing a feast

Wrought-iron chimney crane

Kitchen living-room

Toaster

Open fires in the fireplaces, with roasting jacks turning, the clatter of pewter and earthenware, the bustle of the cooks—these were the sights and sounds in the great kitchens on feast days.

Meals were lavish in summer when food was plentiful, meagre in winter when food was scarce. In poor homes the kitchen was part of the living-room. Cooking utensils were treasured heirlooms.

Living-room of a well-to-do burgher

Spring driven clock

Living-Rooms

Rushlight holder

Carved oak armchair

WL 1596

S FI

Turkish jug with
English silver mounts

Full place setting for one at dining tab

Green glass
flask

In mansions there were beautiful vases, silver, china and cutlery that had been brought from overseas. The Elizabethans made full use of the oak they took from their forests. There was oak panelling round the rooms, grand oak staircases with carved newel posts. The furniture was heavy and made to last. Many items of table-ware were made of pewter.

Open court cupboard

Silver bell salt

Baby's chair

Farmhouse table

Two-handled tyg or drinking cup

Pewter cup

Pewter spoon

Sideboard

Steel knife

Much of the furniture was heavily carved. As wood was cheap and easily obtained, even the poor cottagers had some strong oak furniture. They also had earthenware pottery and wooden cutlery.

Italian potters from Antwerp settled in England during Elizabeth's reign. At this time, too, a royal privilege and monopoly was granted to a **Venetian** glass-maker. From this time these crafts developed. 33

Bedrooms

Palliasse

Day bed

Staircase at Knole

Farmhouse bedroom

Canopied bed

Cradle

Low-raftered and dimly lit by rush or candle-light, the bedrooms were often gloomy and cold. In the mansions the four-poster beds were hung with richly embroidered drapery. In poorer homes men and women slept on palliasses. The chest was an essential part of the furniture in great houses. It was travelling trunk and seat as well as serving for the storage of clothing and linen

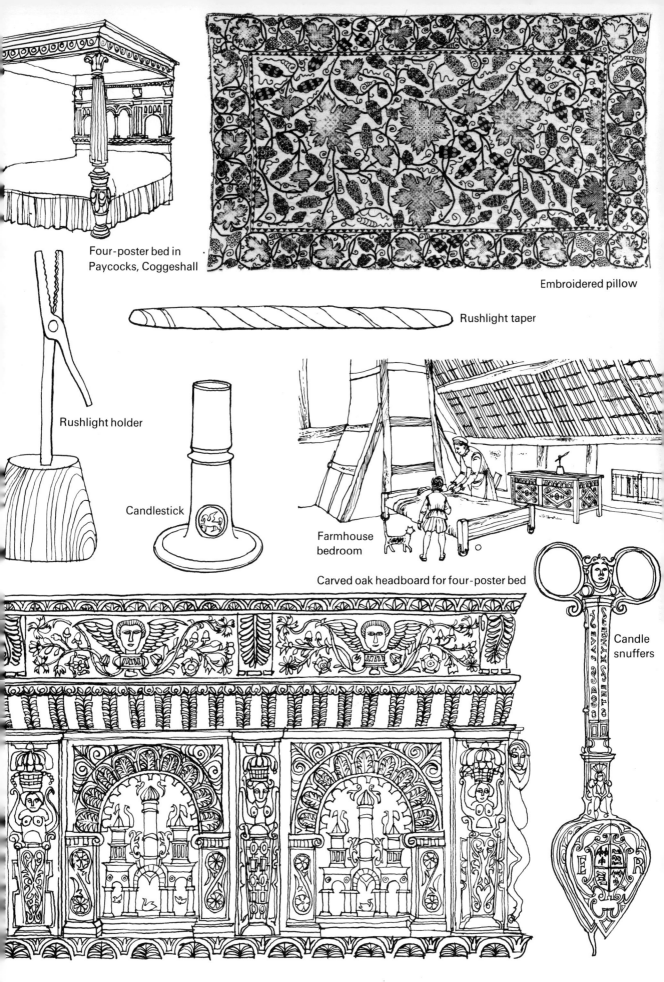

Four-poster bed in
Paycocks, Coggeshall

Embroidered pillow

Rushlight taper

Rushlight holder

Candlestick

Farmhouse
bedroom

Carved oak headboard for four-poster bed

Candle
snuffers

Other items of furniture besides the chest and four-poster bed were joined tables, cupboards, chairs and stools. Despite acts passed to encourage the growing of flax for linen, rich people preferred to buy rich fabrics from the Continent. Embroidering was a woman's occupation. Many great ladies were skilled needlewomen, including Mary, Queen of Scots, and Queen Elizabeth herself.

Funeral of Sir Philip Sidney

Holy-days and Holidays

Preaching at St Paul's Cross

Queen Elizabeth hawking

Hobby-horses

Pick-a-back fights and leap-frog

Folk-dancing to music played on the pipes

Will Kempe morris dancing to Norwich

The holy-days were still the holidays. There were the twelve days of Christmas with fun and jollity led by the elected Lord of Misrule. At Whitsun ale was drunk from the great flagons in the church.

On the eve of May Day the young people brought the maypole from the woods, decorated it and then danced round it with the fiddler playing merrily. The Elizabethans worked hard, but they played hard, too.

Landmarks in civilization, 1558 to 1603

1558 Anthony Jenkinson, an Englishman, explored the Caspian Sea region searching for a new route to China.

1559 Titian painted his famous picture *Diana and Actaeon*.

1560 Brueghel the Elder, a Flemish artist, painted *Children's Games*.
John Knox began writing the treatises which formed the basis for Scottish Presbyterianism.
Sir Thomas Gresham began currency reform: stated 'Gresham's Law' which says that bad money tends to drive good money out of circulation.
Jean Nicot imported tobacco into France.
Scientific Society was founded at Naples.

1561 The first English historical tragedy was produced: *Gorboduc* or *Ferrex and Porrex* by Sackville and Norton.
Fallopius, carrying out research on women's reproductive organs, discovered the tubes in the female anatomy which are named after him.

1562 Benvenuto Cellini, an Italian goldsmith and sculptor, began his *Autobiography*, a bragging account of his adventures.
Tintoretto, whose real name was Jacopo Robusti, painted *Christ at the Sea of Galilee*.
Veronese painted *Marriage at Cana*.
Sir John Hawkins, British sailor, made his first voyage to the West Indies.
Slave trade in West Africa began.

1563 John Foxe's *The Book of Martyrs* was published. Originally called *Actes and Monuments*, the book described the sufferings of Christian martyrs.
Ambrose Paré, the French surgeon to King Henry II, and the son of a barber, published his *Five Books of Surgery*, which helped to establish surgery as a medical science.
Bernard Palissy, a French potter who had experimented for many years in ceramics, began making his famous dishes.

1564 Michelangelo worked on a sculpture *Rondanini pietà* until his death which occurred in his ninetieth year. This Florentine sculptor is one of the great figures in the Renaissance.
Horse-drawn coaches were introduced into Britain from Holland.

1565 Three famous pictures painted in this year were Brueghel's *Autumn and Winter*, Titian's *Toilet of Venus* and Tintoretto's *Crucifixion*.
Hawkins introduced sweet potatoes into England, and tobacco was possibly brought to England for the first time.

1566 One of the world's first newspapers, *Notizie Scritte*, was issued in Venice.
Sir Thomas Gresham founded the Royal Exchange in London.

1567 *Tallis's Canon* composed. Two Welsh achievements in the same year were Gruffydd Robert's *Welsh Grammar* and a translation of the New Testament into Welsh by Salesbury and Davies.
Rio de Janeiro was established in Brazil.

1569 El Greco's *Coronation of a Saint or a King* demonstrated the skill of the Cretan painter, Domenikos Theotokopoulos, who worked in Spain.

1569 Gerhardus Mercator invented the Mercator map projection (showing the round world as a flat map). He originated the term *Atlas* for a set of maps.

1570 Palladio, an Italian architect, published *Treatise on Architecture*. He was the first architect to treat buildings as part of the landscape. His work influenced Sir Christopher Wren.

1571 Harrow School and Jesus College, Oxford, founded.
Leonard Digges constructed the theodolite, an instrument used by surveyors to measure angles and directions.

1572 First Parish Poor Rate: a compulsory levy on each parish to relieve the poor.

1575 *Gammer Gurton's Needle*, first English comedy, produced. Author unknown.
Torquato Tasso wrote his masterpiece *Jerusalem Delivered*, an epic poem about the Crusades and the delivery of the sacred tomb.

1576 Tycho Brahe, a Danish astronomer, established an observatory at Uraniborg.
First English theatre was opened, at Shoreditch.

1577 Sir Martin Frobisher made the second of his three attempts to reach Asia by means of a North-west Passage.
Holinshed's *Chronicles*, which were used by Shakespeare to provide plots for his plays, published.

1579 A survey carried out by Saxton provided Britain with her first atlas.
John Lyly wrote *Euphues*, which set a pattern for an exaggerated and artificial style of writing.

1580 Earliest reference to *Greensleeves*, an old and popular melody.
Last miracle play was performed in Coventry.

1581 Drake returned from his voyage round the world.
Galilei said to have observed the properties of the pendulum.
Ballet Comique de la Reyne by Beaujoyeux, performed at Versailles: probably the world's first ballet.

1582 Hakluyt's *Voyages* written: provided an account of British exploration.
Teatro Olimpico, claimed to be the first theatre, built in Vicenza.

1583 First life assurance policy issued.

1584 Von Grafenberg introduced artificial respiration.

1585 Raleigh attempted to establish an English colony in America: called Virginia after Elizabeth 'The Virgin Queen'.

1587 Christopher Marlowe wrote *Tamburlaine:* a play which influenced later drama with its concentration on a heroic figure.
Banco di Rialto, the world's first modern bank, was founded in Venice.

1589 Rev. William Lee invented the first knitting machine because, it is said, his wife paid more attention to her knitting than to him.

1590 Three famous epic poems written: Sidney's *Arcadia*, Marlowe's *The Jew of Malta* (in dramatic form) and Spenser's *Faerie Queene*.
Galileo made first experiments with falling bodies and published *De Motu*.

1592 John Davis discovered Falkland Islands.
Marlowe wrote *Dr Faustus*: killed in a brawl a year later.

1593 Shakespeare wrote *A Midsummer Night's Dream*.
Final abolition of bows and arrows as weapons of war.
Raleigh went to Guiana in search of El Dorado.

1597 Rinuccini's *La Dafne*, the world's first opera, produced.
Dutch founded Batavia in the Pacific.
Survivors of Willem Barents' expedition to the Barents Sea, north of Norway, returned to Amsterdam.

1598 Admiral Yisunsin of Korea invented first iron-clad warships to defeat the Japanese.
Ben Jonson's *Every Man in His Humour* written.

1599 Globe Theatre, in which many of Shakespeare's plays were performed, built in Southwark, London.
Swiss scientist, Konrad von Gesner, laid foundations of modern zoology.

1600 William Gilbert's *De Magnete* published: described magnetic field and introduced names such as 'electricity'.

1601 Fermat laid the foundation of theories of numbers and numeration.
John Donne, the Dean of St Paul's in his later years, wrote *Progress of the Soul*, a metaphysical poem.

1602 Foundation of the Dutch East India Company.

1603 Fabrizio made the first accurate drawings of valves in veins.
De Champlain explored St Lawrence River.

Early Stuarts
1603-1660

Consultant Historian: John D. Bareham, BA
Designer and illustrator: Leslie Marshall, MSIA

THE STUART DYNASTY divides naturally into two parts:
Early Stuarts *from the accession of King James in 1603 to the restoration of the monarchy in 1660, and* Later Stuarts *from 1661 until the death of Queen Anne in 1714. This is a tragic story of obsession with religious differences and the power of the monarchy. The Stuarts' interest in the British throne began with the conspiracies of Mary Queen of Scots and ended with the holocaust of Culloden. But the lives of the citizens and peasants in Stuart England were mainly untouched by the extremes of tragedy and romance. The rivalry of Protestant and Catholic, Crown and Parliament was woven into the tapestry of history; the commoners' domestic hardships and struggles, achievements and failures belonged to a rougher canvas.*

'real tennis'

party at the Duke of Newcastle's House 1656

Sports and amusements

gambling

James, Duke of York, playing tennis 1640

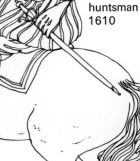
flying a kite

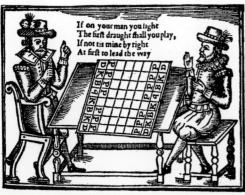
chess

hunting

huntsman 1610

Even the Puritans could not deny the citizens and peasants their sports and pastimes. Despite long hours in the fields, peasants participated in the vigours of morris dancing. The arrival of the dancing bear was a rare and exciting event in village life; the baiting of the bull in the bull-ring a time for gambling. The Court amusements were more sophisticated. Royal or real tennis, played on indoor courts, was a favourite game

making apple fritters
round the fire

dancing round
the maypole

bull-baiting

ballad-singer

morris dancers

of King Charles I and his two sons. Battledore and shuttlecock was popular. Chess was a game for intellectuals. King James I brought a game called 'golf' from Scotland. The main outdoor sport for gentlemen was hunting. A hunt even penetrated the battlefield during the Civil War. The huntsmen halloa'ed and carried on their hunt, while the soldiers continued to kill each other.

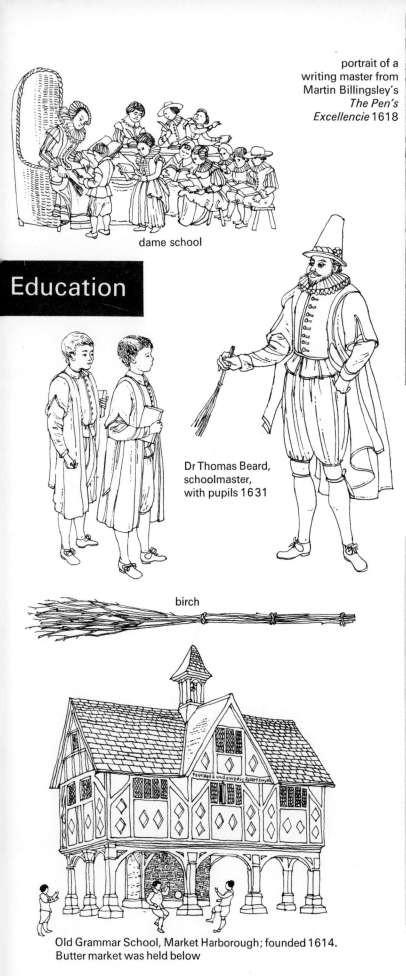

dame school

Education

Dr Thomas Beard, schoolmaster, with pupils 1631

quill pen

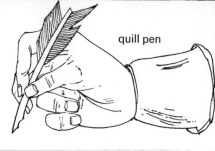

birch

Old Grammar School, Market Harborough; founded 1614. Butter market was held below

sonnet in the hand of James I

The Early Stuart period saw an increased interest in science and medicine. However, the grammar-schools and universities concentrated upon Latin and the classics. King James I was a famous scholar with a variety of interests. He published a book on witchcraft, and appointed fifty-four scholars to make a revision of the Bible.

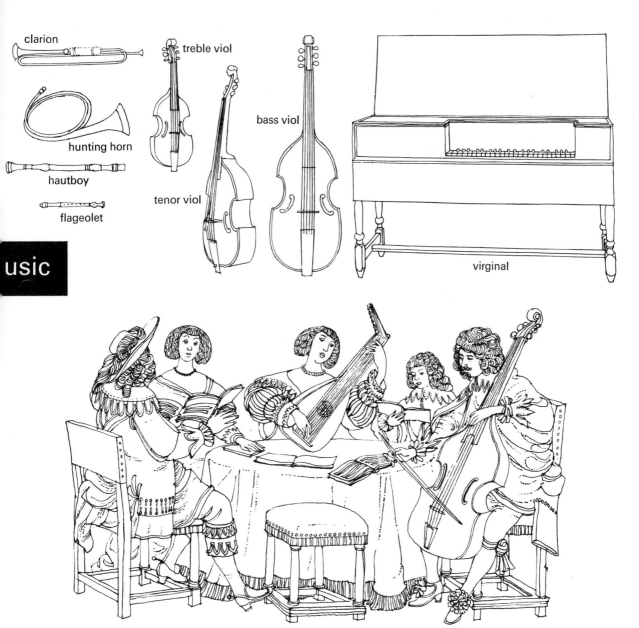

clarion

hunting horn

hautboy

flageolet

treble viol

tenor viol

bass viol

virginal

usic

singers accompanied by lute and bass viol

asque: stage and costumes for allegorical figures designed by Inigo Jones c.1610

William Byrd and Orlando Gibbons continued to compose their sacred and secular music throughout the reign of King James I, and the love of music continued even throughout the Civil War. Organ music was popular, and madrigal singing was a common form of entertainment. Every market town boasted at least one musician of sorts who could accompany the dancers upon his fiddle, his lute or his pipe.

detail from
Inigo Jones's drawing for
the Queen's Chapel,
Somerset House 1623-7

Architecture

Inigo Jones; painting by Hogarth based on
Van Dyck's sketch

part of design by Inigo Jones
for inner court of
Whitehall Palace c.1638

east front of Aston Hall, near Birmingham 1618-35

King Charles's room
at Aston Hall,
and ceiling of
great drawing-room

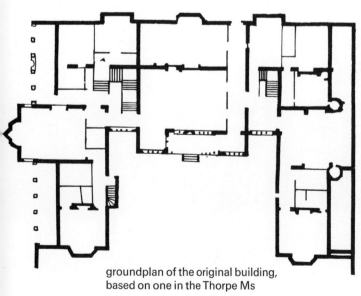
groundplan of the original building,
based on one in the Thorpe Ms

There can be no sudden changes in architecture.
Many seventeenth-century buildings repeat the
characteristics of Elizabethan architecture. Gradually
the classical style was developed. The foremost

exponent of this style was Inigo Jones, whose
Banqueting Hall in the King's palace of Whitehall was
an outstanding example of his art. Inigo Jones began
as a painter before he came under the influence of the

Inigo Jones's preliminary design for
the Banqueting House, Whitehall

original capital from
the Banqueting House

Queen's House, Greenwich;
Inigo Jones 1610-35

brick chimneys

long gallery at
Astley Hall, Lancashire

Raynham Hall, Norfolk,
built in the Dutch style 1635

architect Andrea Palladio in Italy. As royal architect
for King James I, he dominated the architectural scene in
Britain. Architects followed him and copied his style.
Well-proportioned buildings with sashed windows,

pillars and wide cornices are characteristic of this
period, as are the ornamental mouldings between
floors and near the roof. Unfortunately the Civil War
interrupted this growth in fine buildings.

Theatre and the arts

1 Francis Bacon
2 John Donne
3 Ben Jonson
4 Anthony Van Dyck

play at the Middle Temple Hall

title page of Ben Jonson's works

the Earl of Southampton,
patron of the theatre

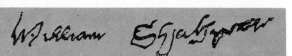

William Shakespeare

drawing by Henry Peacham of an early production of 'Titus Andronicu'

Shakespeare was still composing his plays during the reign of King James I, and the Globe Theatre was in use until 1644. Ben Jonson's plays and the comedies of Beaumont and Fletcher were produced during this period, and Donne and Milton were already writing. But in 1642 an ordinance of the Long Parliament closed places of entertainment. For the next twenty years Puritanism stifled the arts.

Calicut, India

the colonies

Powhatan's cloak of deerskin decorated with shells

Captain John Smith, first governor of Virginia and founder of Jamestown 1607

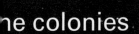
...um – money used for trading in New England

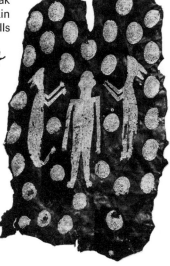

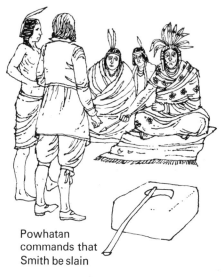
Powhatan commands that Smith be slain

...ers emigrating to America

East India House, Leadenhall Street; built 1648

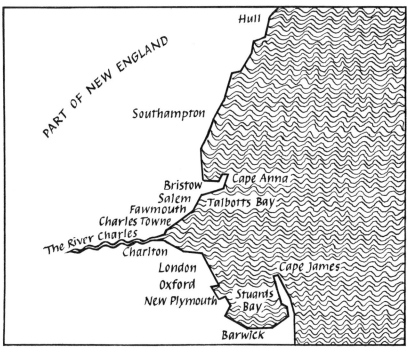

PART OF NEW ENGLAND

Hull

Southampton

Bristow
Salem
Fawmouth
Charles Towne
The River Charles
Cape Anna
Talbotts Bay
Charlton
London
Oxford
New Plymouth
Stuards Bay
Cape James
Barwick

New England; after John Smith's map

Sir Walter Raleigh dreamt of colonies in America. His plans failed. In 1607 a group of settlers led by Captain John Smith tried once more in Virginia. After early struggles the colony survived. In 1620 the *Mayflower* sailed to the New World with the Pilgrim Fathers, whose colony in Massachusetts was to attract 20,000 more Puritans by 1640. Meanwhile the East India Company was setting up its 'factories' in India.

nocturnal used in navigation c.1646

Ships and shipping

terrestrial globe
by Molyneaux

four seamen tail on to shorten sail before a gale

Mayflower in which the Pilgrim Fathers
sailed to the New World in 1620

King James I executed Raleigh because he attacked the
Spaniards in his expedition to South America. Shipping
had been allowed to deteriorate so much since
Elizabethan times that when an attack was made upon

Cadiz, the ships were rotten and the men untrained.
The remnants of the fleet returned to Plymouth, beaten
and disgraced. Meanwhile pirates, aware of their
immunity from danger, plundered ships even in the

Sovereign of the Seas, the largest and best armed warship of the period, extravagantly decorated with gilded carving 1637

dividers

detail of chart of Thames estuary 1612

climbing the rigging to the crow's nest

English Channel. Charles I sought to extend the ship tax and met opposition from Parliament that helped to precipitate the Civil War. Cromwell strengthened the fleet. Robert Blake destroyed the Royalist fleet led by Prince Rupert. Then came a series of victories against the Dutch under Tromp and the Spanish fleet off Tenerife. The one great ship in this period of naval recuperation was the *Sovereign of the Seas.*

blacksmiths

Science and industry

lock of steel, chiselled, pierced and engraved

Gascoigne's screw micrometer

winding off silk

plating mill with
three small hammers
moved by one wheel

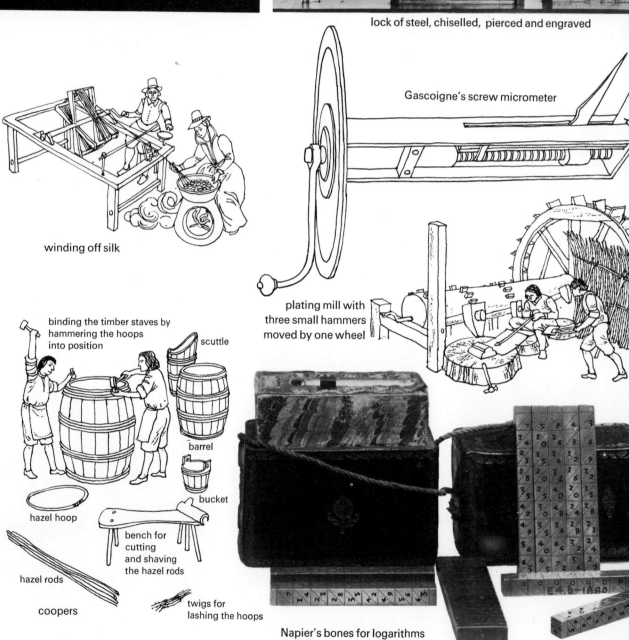

binding the timber staves by
hammering the hoops
into position

scuttle

barrel

bucket

hazel hoop

bench for
cutting
and shaving
the hazel rods

hazel rods

coopers

twigs for
lashing the hoops

Napier's bones for logarithms

In 1605 Francis Bacon produced *The Advancement of Learning* in which he pleaded for the recognition of science. Bacon was not a great scientist, but he championed, and therefore helped, scientific progress.

The outstanding scientific discovery of the Stuart age was William Harvey's observations on the circulation of blood. John Napier, a Scottish mathematician, can be said to have contributed to modern mathematical

...thecary arrives to
...inister a douche

apothecary's shop

fleeing from the plague

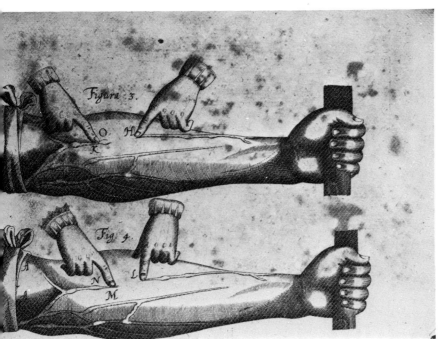

...stration of an experiment demonstrating the circulation of the blood 1612

title page of a book of anatomy 1638

teaching. In *Canonis Descriptio,* published in 1614, he described the system of logarithms. He invented 'bones' or rods for multiplying and dividing, and for extracting square and cube roots. He also introduced formulas for spherical trigonometry. The invention of the telescope led to the need for an instrument to measure small angles, and this was the achievement of William Gascoigne, a Yorkshireman.

Town life

confectioner

smith

tailor

shoemaker

saddler

porter

box-maker

soap boiler

glover

meal-man

chicken man

button maker

The towns bustled with trade and authority. They quickly reflected, too, national prosperity or otherwise. Therefore a slump in trade which came in the 1620s was soon reflected in town life. The wars against France and Spain affected activity in the ports. Poor harvests in 1630 and 1631, which increased grain prices, added to the cost of living. Men who had grumbled about their long hours of work suddenly found themselves without

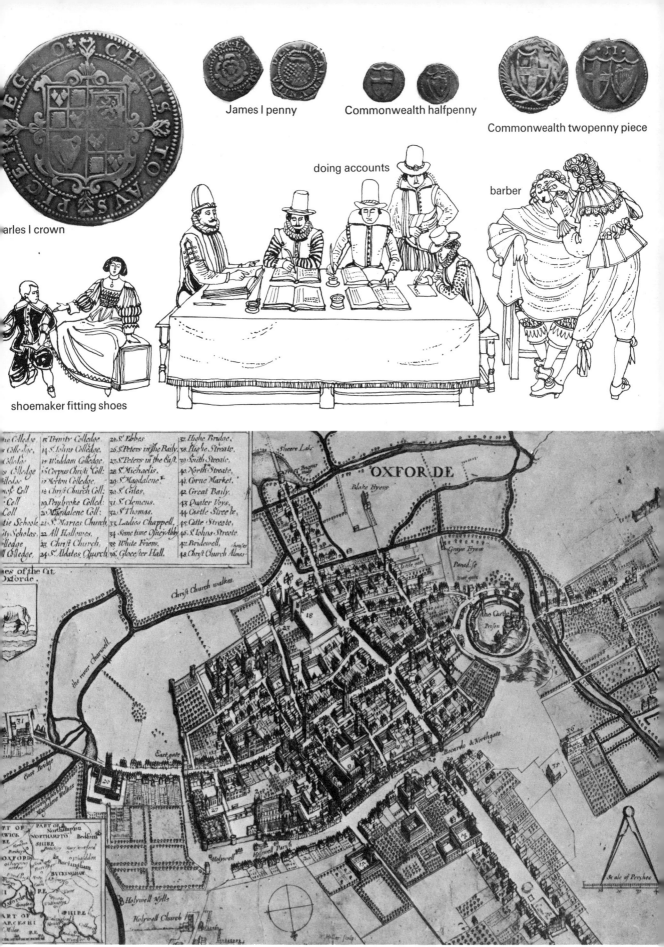

James I penny

Commonwealth halfpenny

Commonwealth twopenny piece

Charles I crown

doing accounts

barber

shoemaker fitting shoes

Oxford in Charles I's time; engraving by Hollar

employment. Poverty combined with Puritanism roused sullen passions of discontent. Neglect in the care of town streets and buildings encouraged the recurring epidemics of plague. Then came the Civil War.

Armaments were needed, resulting in work and prosperity for some. Towns were besieged, and this meant destruction and increased poverty for many people.

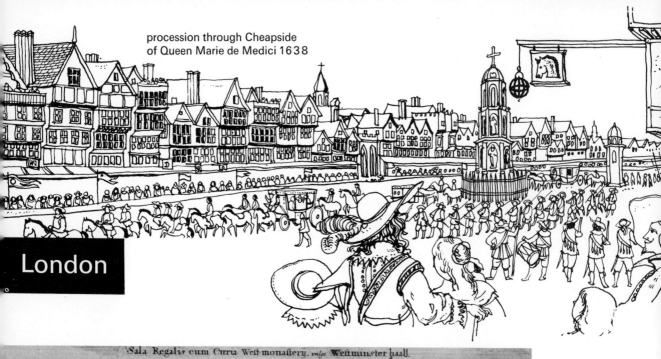

procession through Cheapside
of Queen Marie de Medici 1638

London

Sala Regalis cum Curia Westmonasterij, vulgo Westminster haall.

New Palace Yard, with Westminster Hall and the Clock House; etching by Hollar

1	Old St Paul's
2	Whitehall
3	Somerset House
4	St Clement's
5	Temple
6	Bow Church
7	Guild Hall
8	London Bridge
9	St Dunstan in the East
10	Billingsgate
11	Tower of London
12	St Marie Overis
13	Winchester House
14	The Globe
15	Bear Garden
16	The Swan
17	Hampstead
18	Highgate

London skyline before the Great Fire

THAMESIS FLVVIVS

The dividing line in the history of London is the Great Fire which ravaged much of it in 1666. Until that date London had changed little since Elizabethan days except for the expansion that was taking place outside the city walls. London was the heart of national life. Within the walls were crowded the houses and warehouses of the merchants. Here the Lord Mayor and his aldermen ruled. Here, too, were the City

Old St Paul's, with Inigo Jones's portico of 1633

Banqueting Hall, Whitehall 1619-22

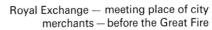

Royal Exchange — meeting place of city merchants — before the Great Fire

companies developed from the Guilds. To the east was the Tower of London; to the west, Westminster with its abbey and palace. The river was still the main thoroughfare. The only bridge across the busy water was the famous London Bridge with its tall houses and shops. Outside the city walls across the river were the taverns, theatres, bear gardens, bull-rings and gardens.

postboy 1647

riding pillion

hackney coach

stage-wagon

Travel

pedlar

ferryman

Ego, non sum Ego.

VERA ET VIVA EFFIGIES CLAUEL GENEROSI ÆTATIS Suæ 25. IOHANNIS

*That I may neither beare anothers blam
Through wronge suspicions nor yet act
At any time hereafter, but prove true
Loe to be knowne your haue my face at*

John Clavel – highwayman 1628

wealthy family's travelling coach;
the framework is elaborately covered in leather

Making use of the posthouses and fresh relays of horses, the King's Messenger brought the news of his accession to James at Edinburgh in three days from London. Acts were passed to make rivers navigable, but they had limited success. Cromwell urged the use of broad-wheeled carts, and he managed to get surveyors of highways appointed in all parishes able to raise a shilling rate and hire labourers.

swimming a witch

debtor's prison

bilboes to which sailors were shackled

poverty, crime and punishment

nding in a pillory

tongue pieces for brank

scold's brank

whipping a vagabond at the cart's end

The Orphans Cry, We perish, we die.

For the Lords sake

Some pity take

Let not this sin to their charge

As we you see
So may yours bee.

I am sick, I die

Dead in the street

or children in the streets,
S. Hartlib 1650

execution of the Gunpowder Plot conspirators

A Poor Law act of 1601 established the system for dealing with the poor – victims of unemployment and poor harvests. The parish administrated. The aged and infirm were cared for in almshouses. Healthy beggars were whipped and returned to their native parish. For the peasant the pillory and stocks remained the chief threat. For the conspirator there was the rack, the thumbscrew and the threat of the stake and quartering.

57

preaching in and out of doors

Religion

Quakers' meeting; contemporary satirical print

christening 1624

clergyman
1642

congregation of the Commonwealth period

title page of first edition of
The book of common prayer.
The reading of this new book
in 1637 led to a riot in
St Giles, Edinburgh

THE
BOOKE OF
COMMON PRAYER,
AND
ADMINISTRATION OF THE
Sacraments.

And other parts of divine Service for
the use of the CHURCH of
SCOTLAND.

EDINBURG
Printed by *Robert Young*, Printer to the
Kings most Excellent Majest.
M.DC.XXXVII.
CUM PRIVILEGIO.

destruction of Cheapside cross by Puritans 1643

There were Puritans in Elizabeth's reign. Numbers increased during the reigns of James and Charles. The division between Anglicans and Puritans widened with the appointment of Laud as Archbishop of Canterbury. He believed that all Englishmen should belong to the national church. The harsh measures he employed, and Charles condoned, increased the rift and the certainty of Civil War.

Parliamentarian helmets

Royalist standard of Lord Lucas

colonel of a regiment

rapier, early seventeenth century

musketeer on the march

Soldiers and arms

Royalist general's riding accoutrements

drummer

caliver-man

infantry officer

musketeer giving fire

pikeman in time of James I

siege battery with artillerists at work

Despite the use of cannon, artillery was a negligible force in the Civil War. The cavalry charged and manoeuvred, but in most battles victory was achieved when the infantry drove the enemy from the field.

The cavalry were mainly gentlemen and farmers who rode their own horses, charging with drawn swords, pistols held in reserve. Infantry were armed with sixteen-foot pikes or muskets.

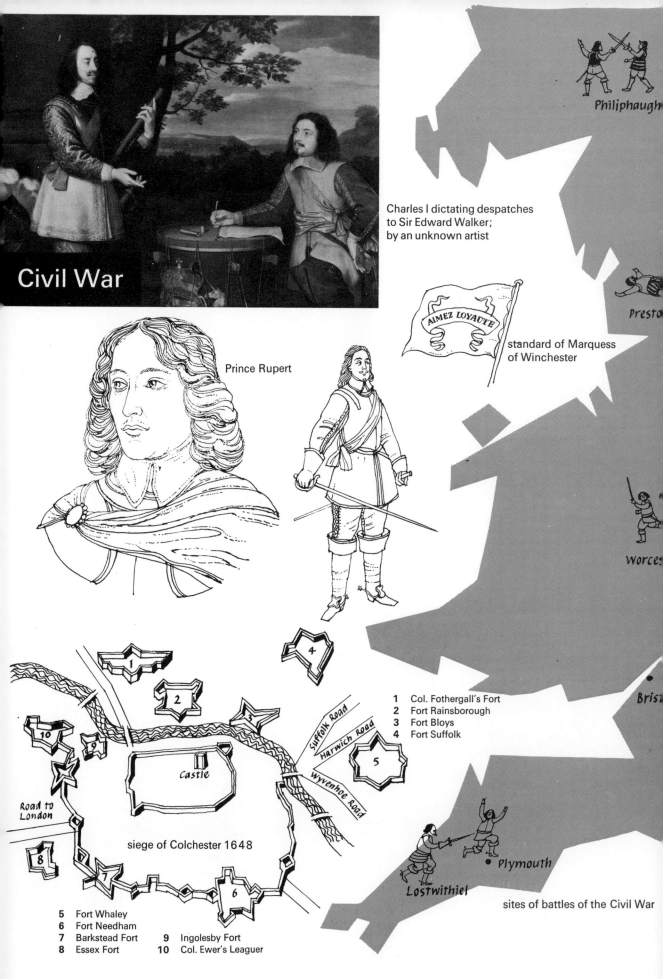

Civil War

Charles I dictating despatches to Sir Edward Walker; by an unknown artist

Philiphaugh

Presto

standard of Marquess of Winchester

Prince Rupert

Worces

1 Col. Fothergall's Fort
2 Fort Rainsborough
3 Fort Bloys
4 Fort Suffolk

Bris

Suffolk Road

Harwich Road

Wyvenhoe Road

Castle

Road to London

siege of Colchester 1648

5 Fort Whaley
6 Fort Needham
7 Barkstead Fort   9 Ingolesby Fort
8 Essex Fort   10 Col. Ewer's Leaguer

Plymouth

Lostwithiel

sites of battles of the Civil War

On August 22nd 1642, the king hoisted his standard at Nottingham. It was harvest-time, with the wet season affording all too little time to harvest the crops. Gentlemen farmers, although sympathetic to the king's cause, gave priority to the harvest. This attitude was to be typical of the way in which the Civil War was fought. There was none of the savage butchery of the Wars of the Roses. In some ways it was a war fought

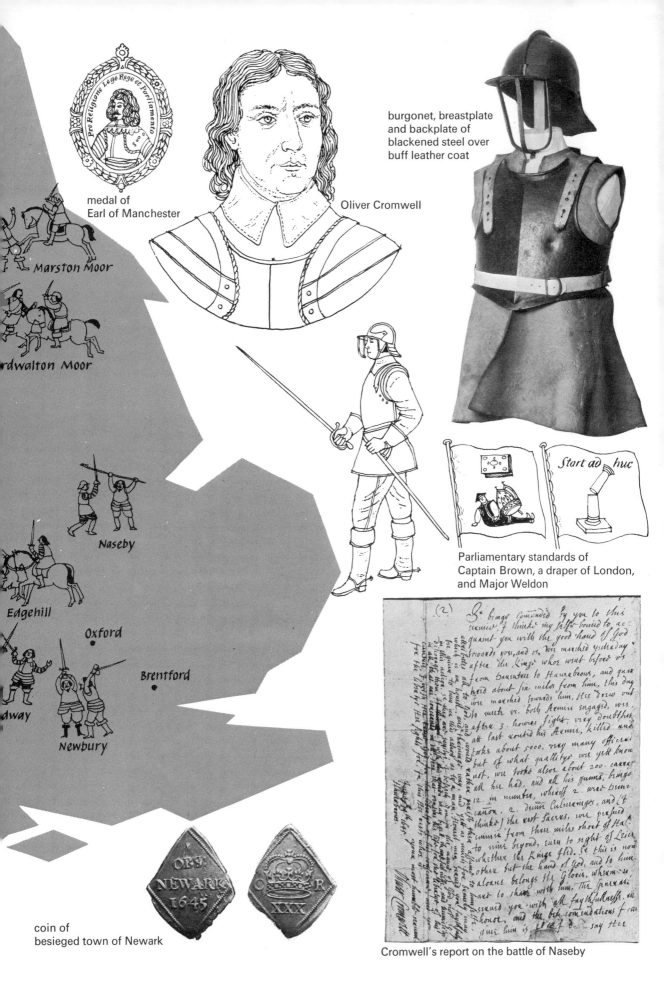

medal of
Earl of Manchester

Oliver Cromwell

burgonet, breastplate
and backplate of
blackened steel over
buff leather coat

Marston Moor

rdwalton Moor

Naseby

Edgehill

Oxford

Brentford

dway

Newbury

Start ad huc

Parliamentary standards of
Captain Brown, a draper of London,
and Major Weldon

coin of
besieged town of Newark

Cromwell's report on the battle of Naseby

by amateurs. Gentlemen fought for the king for a few skirmishes and then went home again. Surrendered garrisons were treated with honour and mercy. Prisoners were allowed to go home after they had promised never to fight again. From April 1645, with the advent of Cromwell's disciplined and professional New Model Army, the defeat of the king's forces was inevitable.

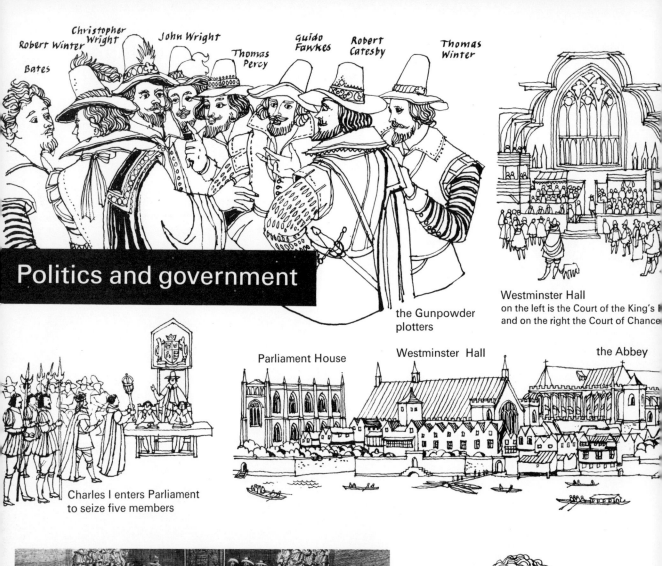

Robert Winter · Christopher Wright · John Wright · Thomas Percy · Guido Fawkes · Robert Catesby · Thomas Winter

Bates

Politics and government

the Gunpowder plotters

Westminster Hall
on the left is the Court of the King's
and on the right the Court of Chance

Charles I enters Parliament
to seize five members

Parliament House · Westminster Hall · the Abbey

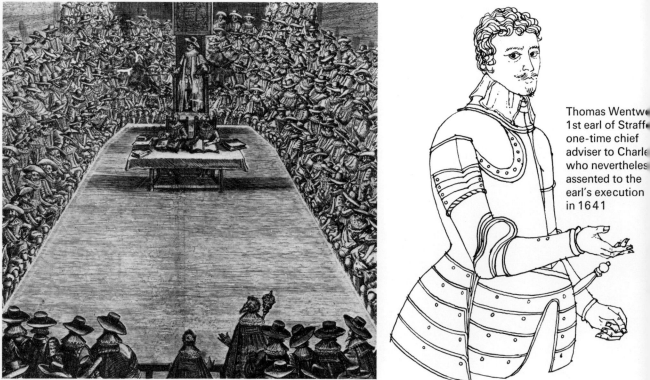

House of Commons 1624

Thomas Wentw
1st earl of Straff
one-time chief
adviser to Charle
who nevertheles
assented to the
earl's execution
in 1641

Who should rule? King Charles I believed in the 'divine right of kings'. Parliament believed that the people's representatives should be the decisive force. The king's position was weakened by his need for money, and the determination of Parliament not to yield to his demands without his meeting their grievances. As Parliament demonstrated its power the king took up the challenge, and the country was embroiled in Civil War. When the

execution of Charles I

Great Seal of Cromwell's Commonwealth

death warrant of Charles I

Cromwell dissolving Parliament 1653

throne was occupied once more, the power of the monarch was never to be the same again. In the country the conflict between Crown and Parliament made little difference to local politics. The Lord-Lieutenant carried out the orders of the central government whoever they were. The real administrators were the Justices of the Peace who supervised poor relief, controlled ale-houses, and maintained roads and bridges.

in a country ale-house

Country life

Bourn post-mill,
Cambridgeshire

cutting a
drainage trench

main street of a village

Sheep-farming was less profitable during the Stuart period than it had been during the Elizabethan age. The Cotswolds lost some of their prosperity. Enclosures did not bring an employment problem as they were now made largely for arable or mixed farming. They did mean more hedges, more specialization and less communal farming projects. A major development was the drainage of the Fens. Vast areas of good land had been regularly

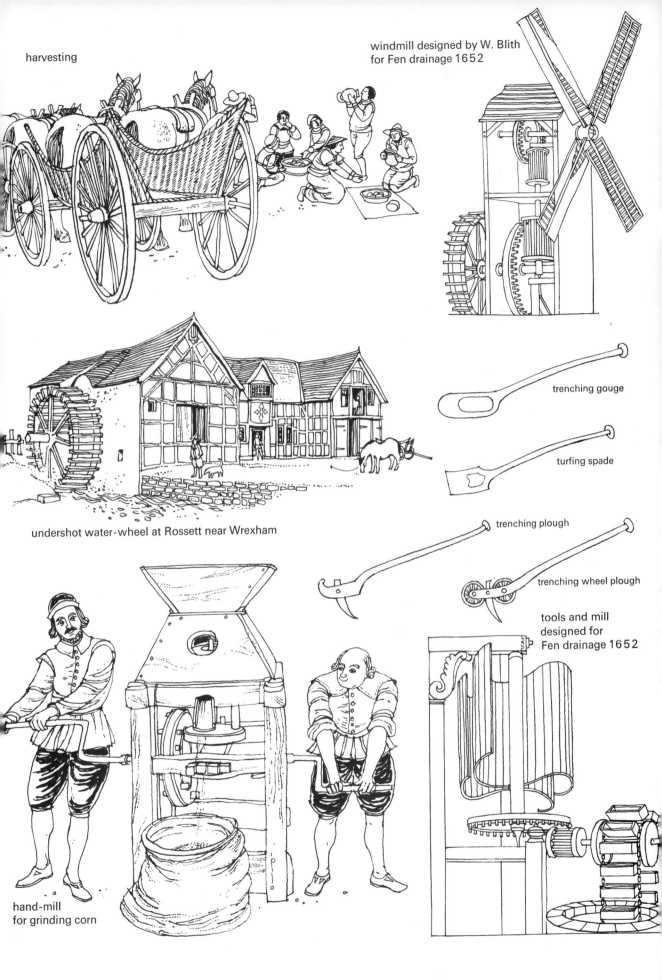

harvesting

windmill designed by W. Blith
for Fen drainage 1652

undershot water-wheel at Rossett near Wrexham

trenching gouge

turfing spade

trenching plough

trenching wheel plough

tools and mill
designed for
Fen drainage 1652

hand-mill
for grinding corn

flooded by the sea or rivers. King Charles I granted a
patent to the Earl of Bedford to drain some 90,000 acres,
and the Dutch engineer Vermuyden was employed.
In other parts of the country changes to the landscape

due to enclosures were gradual. The sails of windmills
still turned, water-wheels clacked, and farming
depended upon the weather. The harvest was still
the most important season in the year.

embroidered cap,
possibly worn by Charles I

lady with muff and stole
nicknamed a 'flea fur' 1639

children in 1635;
the smaller boy is in pettic[...]

Costume

little girl with feather headdress and f[...]
virago sleeves and lace collar 1632

lady of about 1624 wearing cap
called a 'cornet', falling ruff
and embroidered jacket

The clothes worn by Puritans contrasted violently with the Royalist fashions – mainly in the plainness of the untrimmed materials, and even more in the drabness of the colours. Royalists favoured millstone ruffs with long trunkhose. Breeches without padding were known as galligaskins. A characteristic of men's wear in Charles I's reign was the beautiful lace collar. Boots were popular. Women's clothes were freer and not so exaggerated as

ntrywoman and merchant's wife
c.1640

the Duke of Buckingham
in doublet with winged
sleeves 1616

gentleman in cloak-bag
breeches 1625

small boy wearing
adult-style clothes
1626

Charles I with
his sword carried
on a sash, and
wearing wrinkled
boots c.1640

Henrietta Maria's
crimson velvet shoes

es handed to Bishop Juxon by Charles I while on the scaffold

they had been in Elizabeth's time. Bodices were not so rigidly corseted. Petticoats could be glimpsed under gowns looped back with jewelled clasps. Women's riding hats were similar to Cavaliers', large, wide-brimmed,

with plumes. Puritan women had much plainer clothes. They wore white aprons over plain grey or brown gowns. The high black felt hat worn over a white cap still survives in Welsh national costume.

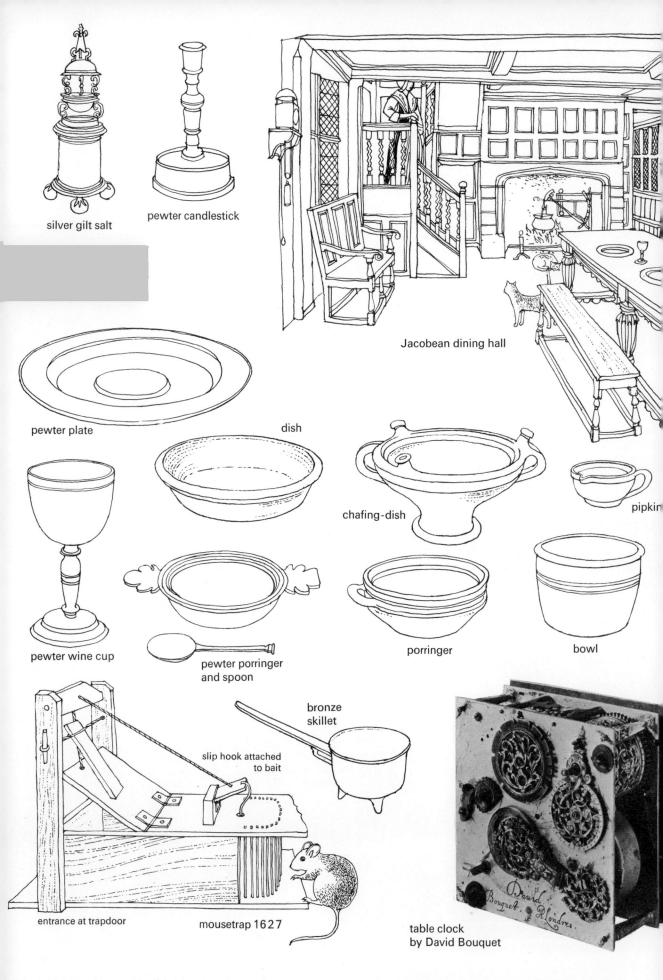

silver gilt salt

pewter candlestick

Jacobean dining hall

pewter plate

dish

chafing-dish

pipkin

pewter wine cup

pewter porringer
and spoon

porringer

bowl

bronze
skillet

slip hook attached
to bait

entrance at trapdoor

mousetrap 1627

table clock
by David Bouquet

Stuart furniture differed little from its Elizabethan
precursors. The main difference was that nearly all
furniture was made smaller so as to be more suitable
68 for the low-ceilinged rooms that were now popular.

The legs of tables and chairs were frequently straight
and not always carved. In the main, however, the
furniture still gave the impression of massiveness and
solidity. Oak was the favourite choice in wood. Puritans

Augsburg-type clock

long gallery

dresser with floral inlay

folding table with one movable gate

cupboard with geometrical inlay

farthingale chair, early 1600s

armchair carved with foliage and scrolls 1660

carved and turned chair 1641

armchair and footstool covered with velvet c.1615

were in favour of simplicity and plainness, and indeed Cromwell banned carving on furniture. One feature indicated the sense of security from wandering bands of robbers. Tables were made wider. Previously they were narrow so that diners could have their backs to the wall and face probable attackers.

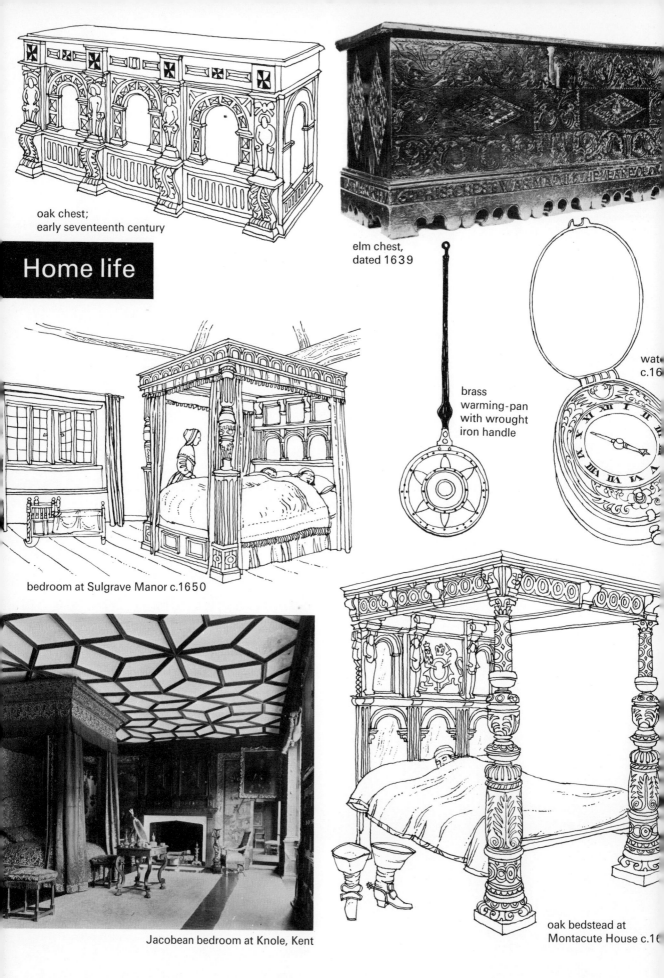

oak chest;
early seventeenth century

elm chest,
dated 1639

Home life

bedroom at Sulgrave Manor c.1650

brass
warming-pan
with wrought
iron handle

wat
c.16

Jacobean bedroom at Knole, Kent

oak bedstead at
Montacute House c.16

As one bedroom opened out of another there was little
privacy outside the curtains of the four-poster bed. With
the curtains drawn the sleeper had privacy and was
given some protection from draughts. Linen sheets, silk

bedspreads, velvet and cloth-of-gold curtains about
the four-posters were far beyond the purse of the
average yeoman. He made do with homespun hessian
curtains and woollen bedclothes.

Landmarks in civilization, 1603 to 1660

1603 Italian scientific society, Accademia dei Lincei, founded in Rome.

1604 Silk manufacture began in England.
Robert Cawdrey's *Table Alphabetical* published: the first English dictionary.
Johannes Kepler, a German astronomer and mathematician, discovered that the eye has a lens which projects images on the retina.
Playwrights and poets, Dekker, Middleton, Drayton and Breton, all active.

1605 Cervantes published the first modern novel *Don Quixote*.
Incorporation of a number of guilds in London, including the Butchers' Company.

1606 Two famous plays written: Shakespeare's *Macbeth* and Jonson's *Volpone*.
Two great paintings: Rubens' *The Circumcision* and El Greco's *The Feast in the House of Simon*.
Royal Charter granted to Virginia Company for colonization.
Torres, a Spanish explorer, discovered the strait between Australia and New Guinea, which is now named after him.

1609 Tin-enamel ware produced at Delft in Holland.
Galileo made a telescope and saw craters on the moon.
Kepler announced the first two Laws of Planetary Motion.
Hudson entered the bay in North America now named after him, in his search for the North-west Passage to Asia.
Strasbourg Relation, the first regularly published newspaper.

1610 Galileo observed Saturn's rings and Jupiter's moons.
Dutch brought tea from China to Europe.

1611 Authorized version of the Bible published.

1614 John Napier's book on logarithms published.
Raleigh's *History of the World* published.

1615 Inigo Jones, influenced by Palladio of Italy, brought Renaissance architecture to Britain.
Champlain explored the Great Lakes in Canada.
Rubber used by the Spaniards in South America.

1616 Inigo Jones built the Queen's House, Greenwich.
George Chapman translated Homer's *Iliad* and *Odyssey*, later admired by Keats.
William Harvey lectured on the circulation of blood.
Cape Horn in South America, named by a Dutchman after the Dutch town Hoorn, was rounded for the first time.
Baffin Bay, part of the Atlantic Ocean between Canada and Greenland, explored by William Baffin, who was searching for the North-west Passage.
Shakespeare died at Stratford-upon-Avon, his birthplace.

1617 Ben Jonson appointed the first Poet Laureate.
Snell, a Dutchman, invented a new method of measuring land.

1618 Raleigh executed, having failed in his mission to find El Dorado.

1619 Inigo Jones built his masterpiece—the Palace of Whitehall.

1620 *Mayflower* with the Pilgrim Fathers sailed to America.

1621 Sir George Calvert attempted to set up colony in Newfoundland.

1622 William Oughtred invented slide-rule.

1623 First folio edition of Shakespeare's plays published.
Patents Law brought in to protect inventors.

1624 Franz Hals painted *The Laughing Cavalier*.
Gunter invented a surveyor's measuring chain (22 yards): the first of its kind.

1625 Johann Rudolf Glauber, a German chemist, prepared a medicinal salt, known afterwards as Glauber's Salt, from sodium sulphate.
Hugo Grotius, a Dutch lawyer, with the publication of *On the Law of War and Peace*, founded international law.
First fire engines used in England.

1626 Dutch founded New Amsterdam (New York).
Francis Bacon wrote an account of an imaginary island he called *New Atlantis*, in which he described many possible inventions.

1628 Diego Velazquez, a Spanish baroque painter, painted *Christ on the Cross*.
William Harvey, the king's physician, published his book which described the function of the heart and blood circulation.

1629 John Milton wrote *On the Morning of Christ's Nativity*, his first great poem.

1632 Shah Jahan built the Taj Mahal as a mausoleum for his favourite wife.

1633 John Donne's poems published posthumously.

1634 Oberammergau Passion Play first performed to celebrate the end of a plague epidemic.
Vermuyden began draining the Fens.

1639 William Gascoigne invented the micrometer, an instrument for measuring small dimensions.
Velazquez painted *The Surrender of Breda (The Lances)*, one of the world's finest historical paintings.

1640 Coke first made from coal.
Stage coaches introduced into England.
John Evelyn began his famous diary.
Pierre Corneille, French playwright, wrote *Horace*.

1642 Rembrandt, a Dutch painter, painted one of the greatest paintings in history, *The Night Watch*.

1643 Torricelli, Italian mathematician and physicist, discovered the principle of the barometer.

1648 Robert Herrick's *Hesperides* was published.
Herrick was an English clergyman and one of the Cavalier poets.

1650 First development of modern harmony in music.
Tea first drunk in England.

1656 Copenhagen's famous observatory opened.
Opera house opened in London.
De Hooch, noted for his Dutch interiors, painted *A Dutch Courtyard*.

1658 Fromanteel made the first English spring pendulum clock.

1660 Samuel Pepys began his diary.
Royal Society founded by King Charles II.
The post of Master of the King's Musick created.
Von Guericke invented a static electricity machine.
Peter Lely, who became court painter, painted *The Ladies of the Lake*.
Jan Vermeer, the Dutch painter, painted *The Cook*.

Later Stuarts
1661-1714

Consultant Historian: John D. Bareham, BA
Designer and illustrator: Leslie Marshall, MSIA

THE LATER STUARTS PERIOD began with the Restoration of the monarchy in 1660, and ended with the death of Queen Anne who, outliving her children, was succeeded by her cousin George, Elector of Hanover. The jubilation that welcomed the freedom from puritanical restrictions was expressed in exaggerated fashions and bawdy comedy in the newly opened theatres. The period began with conflict between Catholic and Protestant, and finished with conflict between Whig and Tory. Led by the Duke of Marlborough, British armies won famous battles on the Continent. Britain gained victories but also suffered her greatest humiliation at sea. From the ashes of a city devastated by plague and fire, arose a finer London. This was a time of innovation and experiment. The first newspapers were issued, machinery was used on the farm, crude steam engines gave a hint of future power, and Sir Isaac Newton solved some of the mysteries of the universe. The first stirrings of the great agricultural and industrial revolutions were making themselves felt.

Sea and ships

1 *head*
2 *forecastle (forepart of ship under main-deck)*
3 *middle gun-deck*
4 *lower gun-deck*

line-of-battle ship *Prince* 1670; model belonging to Pepys

section of British first-rate ship of 1700
She carried an armament of 100 guns, a crew of 850,
and her best speed was about 10 knots.
The length of her keel was 140 feet, her
beam was 50 feet, and the depth of her hold was 20 feet.

5 *orlop (lowest deck, above the hold)*
6 *hold*
7 *upper gun-deck*

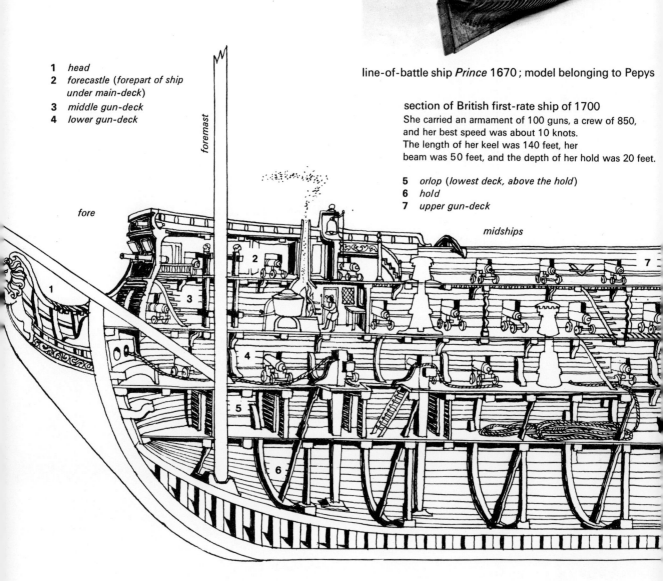

During the early part of the seventeenth century the Dutch became the maritime power in Europe. They took advantage of the Civil War to seize some of Britain's trade. Cromwell aimed to restore Britain's naval power and ensure her foreign trade. He declared war on the Dutch in 1652. Two years and thirteen naval battles later the war was brought to an end. Meanwhile Cromwell's commercial treaties with Sweden had guaranteed access

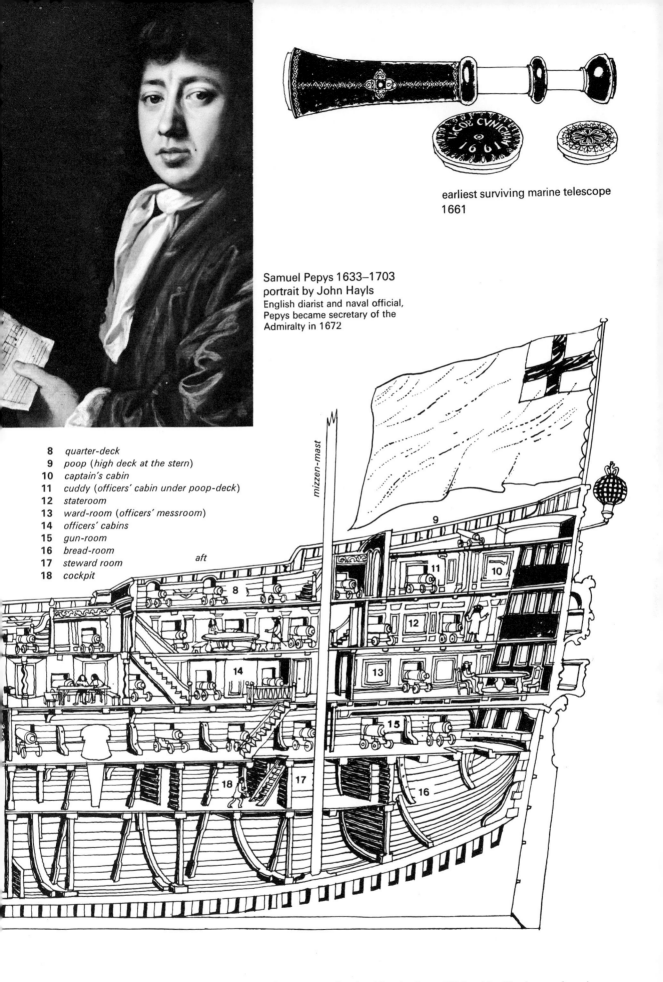

earliest surviving marine telescope
1661

Samuel Pepys 1633–1703
portrait by John Hayls
English diarist and naval official,
Pepys became secretary of the
Admiralty in 1672

8   quarter-deck
9   poop (high deck at the stern)
10 captain's cabin
11 cuddy (officers' cabin under poop-deck)
12 stateroom
13 ward-room (officers' messroom)
14 officers' cabins
15 gun-room
16 bread-room
17 steward room
18 cockpit

mizzen-mast

aft

to Scandinavian timber and other naval supplies. At the
Restoration therefore, King Charles, who was a great
lover of the sea and ships, inherited a fine fleet. For the
first time in British history, the fleet was owned and

maintained by the State. With pride, Charles conferred
the title of Royal Navy upon his fleet. But there was a
penalty to State ownership, which Charles soon realised :
the cost of maintaining the Royal Navy was a problem.

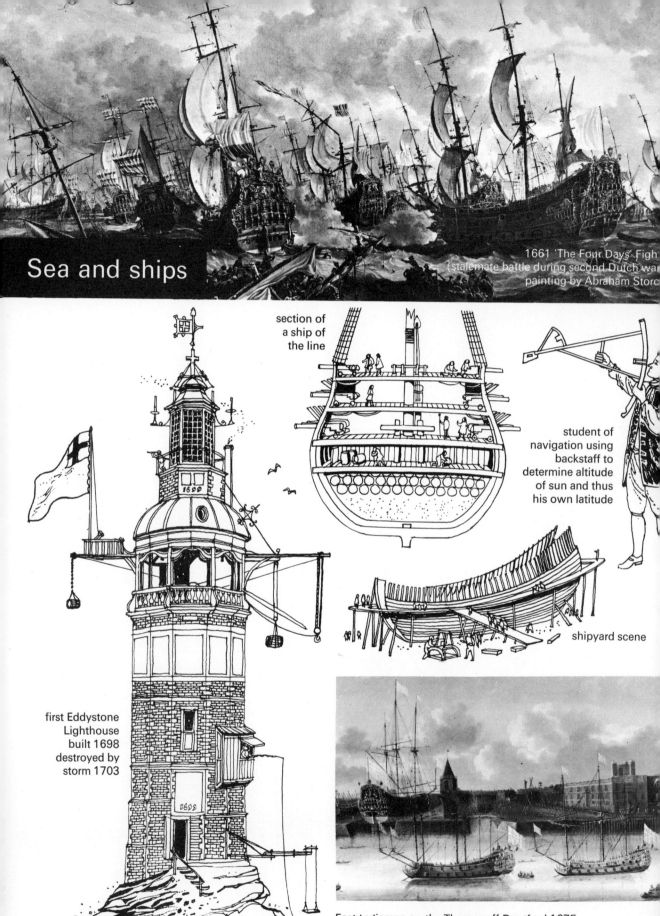

1661 'The Four Days' Fight
(stalemate battle during second Dutch war)
painting by Abraham Storck

section of
a ship of
the line

student of
navigation using
backstaff to
determine altitude
of sun and thus
his own latitude

shipyard scene

first Eddystone
Lighthouse
built 1698
destroyed by
storm 1703

East Indiamen on the Thames off Deptford 1675
painting attributed to Sailmaker

In a second Dutch war, the enemy sailed up the
Thames. Despite the wars, the Secretary of the Admiralty,
Samuel Pepys the diarist, promoted many necessary
reforms. When peace brought the third Dutch War to an
end in 1674, the Royal Navy had fourteen years to
prepare itself for the protracted French wars that began
in 1689.

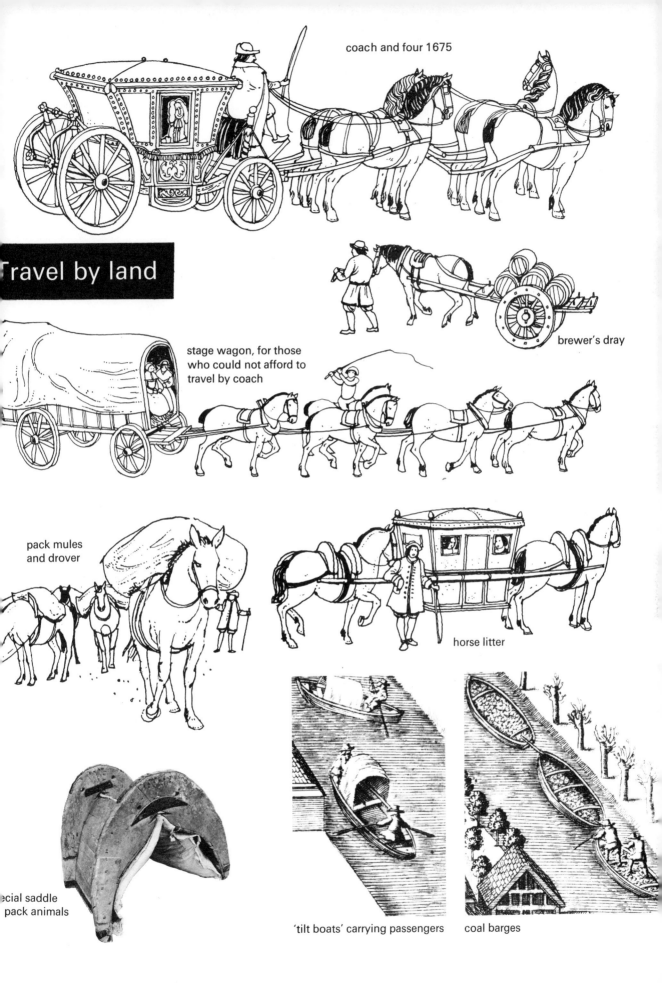

coach and four 1675

brewer's dray

stage wagon, for those who could not afford to travel by coach

pack mules and drover

horse litter

ecial saddle pack animals

'tilt boats' carrying passengers

coal barges

In winter the roads were choked with mud, and in summer deep ruts and holes endangered life and limb. The condition of the roads was mainly due to the law that put the responsibility for road maintenance on each parish. Independent action was taken by some men who built roads and charged travellers to use them, taking tolls at the turnpikes. The rivers were still a main means of communication.

77

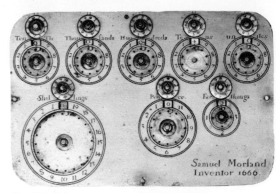

first English calculating machine 1666
devised by Sir Samuel Morland

Science and invention

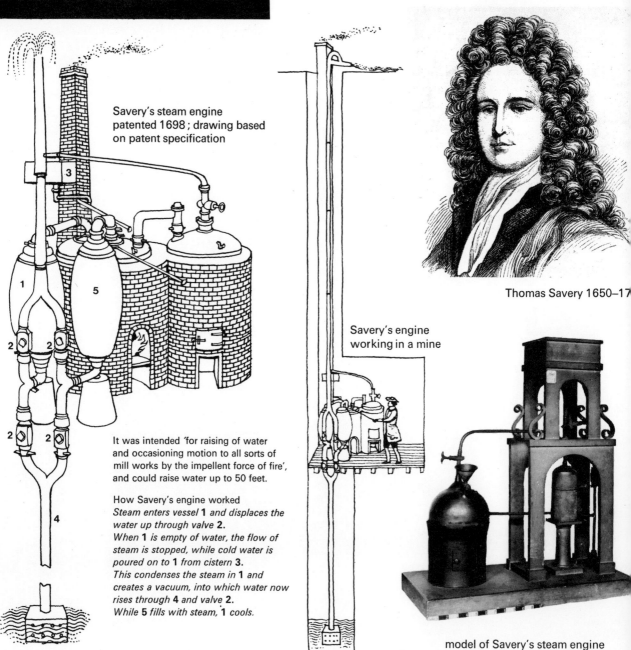

Savery's steam engine
patented 1698 ; drawing based
on patent specification

Thomas Savery 1650–17

Savery's engine
working in a mine

It was intended 'for raising of water
and occasioning motion to all sorts of
mill works by the impellent force of fire',
and could raise water up to 50 feet.

How Savery's engine worked
Steam enters vessel **1** *and displaces the
water up through valve* **2**.
When **1** *is empty of water, the flow of
steam is stopped, while cold water is
poured on to* **1** *from cistern* **3**.
This condenses the steam in **1** *and
creates a vacuum, into which water now
rises through* **4** *and valve* **2**.
While **5** *fills with steam,* **1** *cools.*

model of Savery's steam engine

A group of men who met for experiment and discussion
in Cromwell's time, received King Charles as their patron
and became the Royal Society in 1660. This is the oldest
scientific society in the world and probably the most
famous. Among the members were Robert Boyle, who by
his study of gases made the invention of the steam engine
possible, and Sir Christopher Wren, the architect. An
important member was Edmund Halley, who forecast the

Prince Rupert's fireplace
c. 1678

Newton's reflecting
telescope 1668

Sir Isaac Newton 1642–1727
mathematician and natural
philosopher

replica of seedbox
of Tull's drill

Jethro Tull
1674–1741

Marshall compound microscope c. 1700

In 1701 when the cost of seed rose, Jethro Tull of Berkshire devised an efficient
seed-sowing machine, based on the workings of the organ. The drill cut
furrows for the seeds and sowed them about 2 inches below the surface.

return of the comet now named after him. But the
greatest member was Sir Isaac Newton, mathematician
and discoverer of the principles of gravitation. He also
discovered the secrets of light and colour. He invented a
new branch of mathematics known as calculus.
Preparing the way for the future industrial revolution,
Savery and Newcomen steam pumps entered the mines
in 1712.

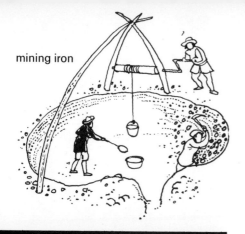

mining iron

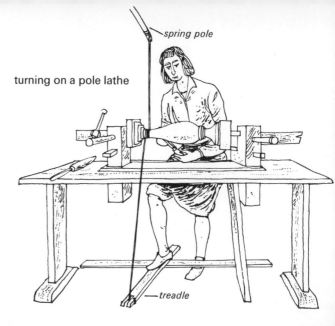

spring pole

turning on a pole lathe

—treadle

S. Nicholls delin: et sculp:

ORDERS AND RULES TO BE OBSERVED BY THOSE WHO SPIN FOR JOHN BURKITT AND COMP.ᴬ

You are to Reele on a full-Yard-reele and reele Eighty Threads in a knot and put three Double knots & one Single one in a Skaine, and if at any time your yarn is found to be reel'd false you are to forfeit all the yarn you bring at that time.

You must not reele two or more Spinners yarn in one Skaine, but each Spinners must be reel'd by it self, And if at any time you are found to have mixed two or more Spinners in one Skaine you must forfeit one penny for every pound you bring at that time over & above the comnion allowance.

You must make your yarn very even. twist it well. and keep it clean.

If at any time you have any yellow wool you must take care you don't mix it with what is whiter but must Spin & reele it by its Self, neither must you mix the yarn of fine & ordinary wool together.

You must not turn your knots on the reele above once, & must not tye them up with Hemp or flaxen thread, but with the yarn you Spin.

You must bring all your wool Spun into yarn every time you come (if Possible) but if you leave any at home it must be an even pound or pounds that so there may be no mistake made by bringing or leaving any less quantity than Pounds.

N.B.   By a late Act of Parliament, all Spinners of Jersey who shall detaine damnify or Spoile any work comitted to their care, or quit or returne the same before its finished are to forfeit double the value of the work so detained Spoiled or return'd to the Master, or be committed to the House of Correction for three Months.

tree-trunk rests on movable carri which is pushed by workman up to spoon-shaped boring tool

The cloth industry was Britain's principal industry and woollen cloth her largest export. Machines, such as the stocking-frame and gig-mill, which had formerly been prohibited, were encouraged but cloth manufacture was still a cottage industry. The iron and steel industry needed charcoal for smelting, because sulphur in coal made metal brittle. But there was a shortage of wood. Then Abraham Darby, the Shropshire ironmaster, introduced a

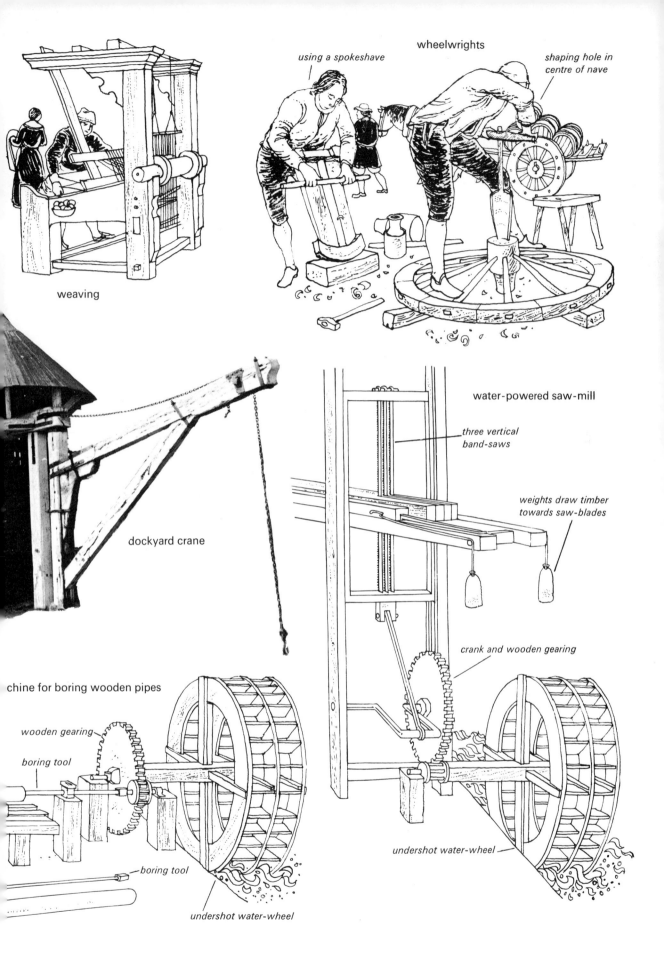

weaving

wheelwrights

using a spokeshave

shaping hole in centre of nave

dockyard crane

water-powered saw-mill

three vertical band-saws

weights draw timber towards saw-blades

chine for boring wooden pipes

wooden gearing

boring tool

crank and wooden gearing

boring tool

undershot water-wheel

undershot water-wheel

successful method of smelting iron with coke and transformed the industry. Deeper seams had to be exploited to get more coal. But agriculture remained the main occupation. At the time of the Restoration turnips were already being grown in Suffolk to provide winter feed for the animals. In Norfolk farmers were experimenting with clover.

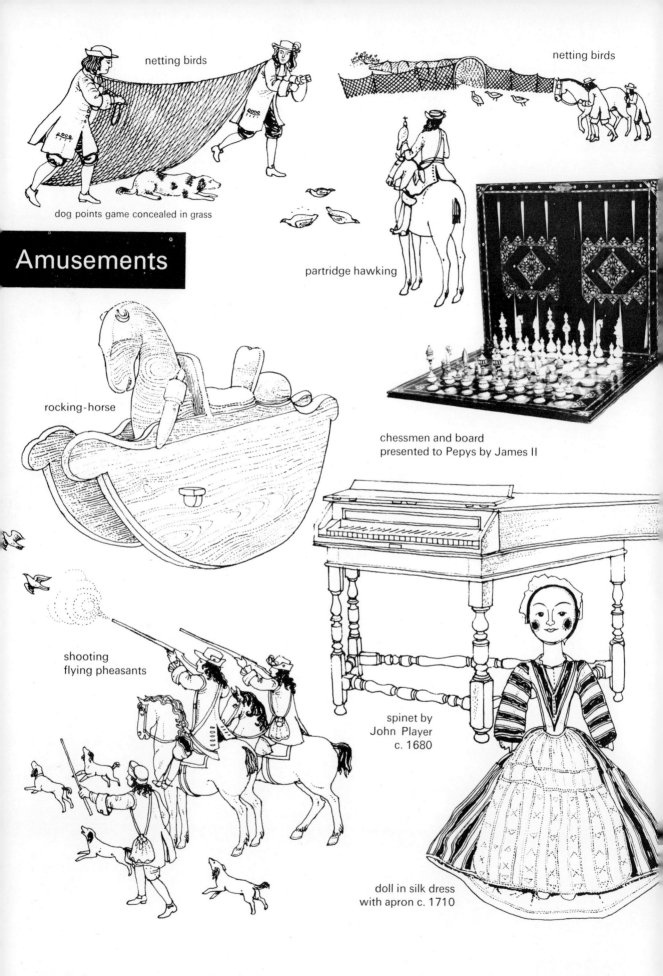

netting birds

netting birds

dog points game concealed in grass

partridge hawking

Amusements

rocking-horse

chessmen and board
presented to Pepys by James II

shooting
flying pheasants

spinet by
John Player
c. 1680

doll in silk dress
with apron c. 1710

The Restoration gave a fresh impetus to dicing and card playing. Chess, draughts and backgammon were played by the staid, but the younger generation preferred fencing and dancing, the fashions of the French court. Bowls, skittles and tennis were popular, and the wealthy enjoyed billiards. Among outdoor sports were fishing, hunting, fowling, falconry, bear-baiting and cock-fighting. Horse-race meetings became a fashion.

Henry Purcell
composer 1659-1695

John Dryden
poet, dramatist
and critic
1631-1700

◀ Godfrey Kneller
portrait painter 1646-1723

◀ William Congreve
playwright and poet
1670-1729

John Vanbrugh
playwright and
architect
1664-1726

he arts

viol player

A scene from Congreve's
comedy *Love for love,* performed at the Old Vic in
1965, with Laurence Olivier,
John Stride, Joyce Redman
and Robert Lang. The play
was first performed in 1695
at the new theatre in
Lincoln's Inn Fields.

'My heart is inditing' by Purcell

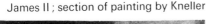

James II ; section of painting by Kneller

The Stuarts were great patrons of the arts, and
influenced the development of taste and morals. Closed
through the Interregnum, theatre doors were
triumphantly flung open in 1660, and the Restoration
comedies of Congreve, Wycherley, Etherege and
Farquhar set London laughing. Portraits and miniatures
retained their popularity. Good music was composed,
notably by Henry Purcell.

yew tree in elaborate topiary work

Gardens

water gardens at Westbury Court, Gloucestershire, laid out c. 1700

Uppark, Sussex c. 1690

presenting first English pineapple to Charles II

yew trees at Owlpen Old Manor, Gloucestershire

from wood carving by Grinling Gibbons, Dutch wood carver who worked for Wren

This was a period of experiment. There was a demand for new vegetables, flowers and fruit. Queen Henrietta herself is said to have introduced jasmine into Britain. New plants, such as nasturtium, honesty and laburnum, were seen. The Dutch influence showed itself in formal gardens, and even more in the popularity of tulips. Clipped yew hedges and decorative statues became a feature.

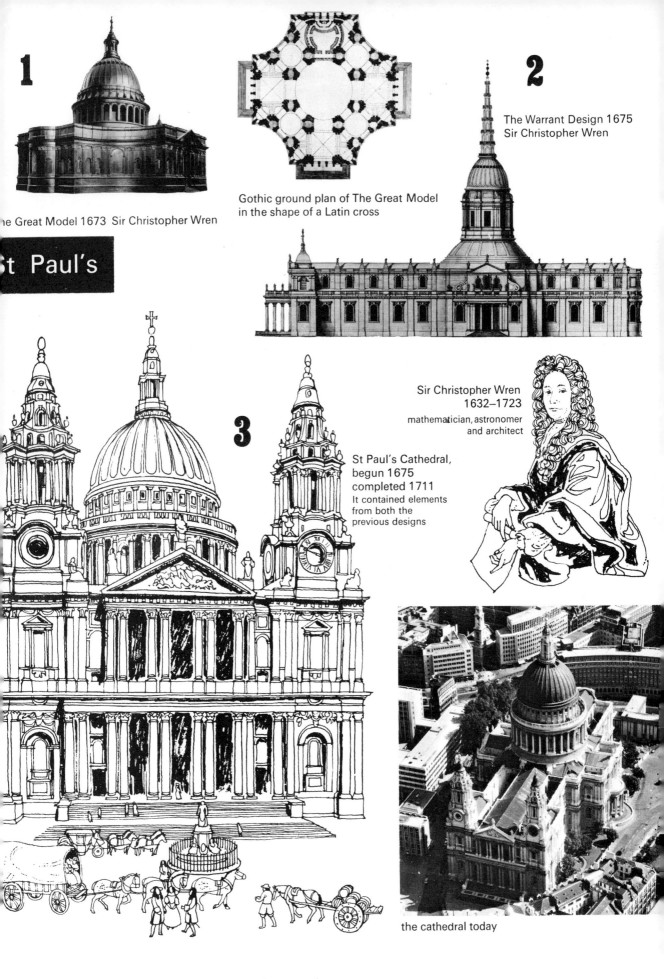

1

The Great Model 1673 Sir Christopher Wren

Gothic ground plan of The Great Model
in the shape of a Latin cross

2

The Warrant Design 1675
Sir Christopher Wren

St Paul's

3

Sir Christopher Wren
1632–1723

mathematician, astronomer
and architect

St Paul's Cathedral,
begun 1675
completed 1711
It contained elements
from both the
previous designs

the cathedral today

As the royal surveyor, Christopher Wren had already planned to rebuild St Paul's Cathedral before the Great Fire of 1666 destroyed it. His first plans were rejected, and the great dome, replacing the mediaeval spire, was not introduced until the final plan. Wren was buried in the crypt in 1723, with the apt epitaph 'Lector, si monumentum requiris, circumspice' (Reader, if you seek his monument, look around you).

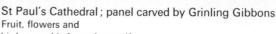
St Paul's Cathedral; panel carved by Grinling Gibbons
Fruit, flowers and
birds were his favourite motifs

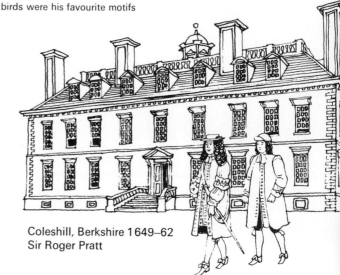
Coleshill, Berkshire 1649–62
Sir Roger Pratt

Architecture

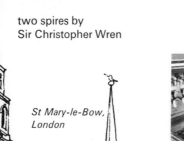
two spires by
Sir Christopher Wren

St Bride,
London

St Mary-le-Bow,
London

The Hall at Coleshill, with Italian influence in design
and decoration

The Sheldonian Theatre, Oxford 1662–3 Sir Christopher Wren

Although Inigo Jones died before Charles II came to the throne, his classical style influenced the work of the Restoration architects. One of the most versatile was Sir John Vanbrugh, who was playwright as well as architect.

His most celebrated achievement is the vast and magnificent Blenheim Palace. The palace was built as a gift from the nation to the Duke of Marlborough for his victories on the Continent. The outstanding architect was

The Crown House, Newport, Essex, once a public house
The pargetted plaster work was added in 1692

The Custom House, London, rebuilt after the fire
Sir Christopher Wren, 1669

Castle Howard, Yorkshire
1699–1712 Sir John Vanbrugh

The Chapel, Chatsworth House, Derbyshire, unchanged since 1694
altarpiece designed by Caius Gabriel Cibber

Sir Christopher Wren. At one time he was professor of mathematics, and at the Restoration, professor of astronomy at Oxford. His first architectural success was the Sheldonian Theatre in Oxford. He prepared a magnificent new city plan for London after the Fire. Land-owners made this impossible, but a number of London churches were built to his plans.

Duke of Albemarle's watermen
and Master of the Barge

chimney-sweep

a brass pot or
an iron pot to mend

long thread laces,
long and strong

buy my Du
biscuits

London life

London after rebuilding

1	St Paul's Cathedral	**4**	London Bridge
2	Royal Exchange	**5**	Billingsgate
3	Fishmongers Hall	**6**	Custom House

London dominated the country more during this period than at any other time. It contained one-tenth of the population and was many times larger than Bristol. It was important as a port, a market, and the seat of government, and the home of the richest merchants in the land. It was also the centre of the developing banking system. Goldsmiths, who had strong-rooms for precious metals, were the first bankers. In 1694 a group of

from Tempest's *Cries of London* 1688–1711

lily-white vinegar

a merry new song

old cloaks,
suits or coats

small coal

new river water

London's Gazette

7 *Tower of London*

8 *The Monument*

London after the Great Fire of 1666, engraving by Hollar

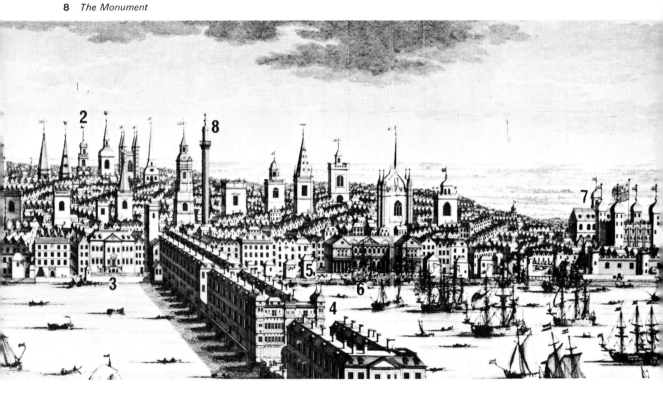

Londoners lent more than a million pounds to the government in return for the right to issue bank-notes. This was the foundation of the Bank of England. The three great disasters—plague, the Great Fire and the breakdown of the Thames defences against the Dutch—were devastating, but London was rebuilt. Streets were wider and some houses built of brick, but many areas remained squalid.

Town life

bathing at Bath 1670s

nonconformist minister

hand-squirt

fire-fighting equipment

leather fire-buckets

fireman's helmet

fire-mark of Sun
Insurance Office 1711
on house in Fulham

After the Great Fire,
citizens took fire
precautions more seriously

838

fire-engine

The Court was at Whitehall and was a world in itself.
Here, fashionably-dressed courtiers intrigued, gossiped,
paraded and amused themselves. The tittle-tattle of
State affairs was bought and sold for personal
advancement or sheer curiosity. Not far away, in
Westminster, rich citizens lived comfortable lives away
from the infections and squalor of the rest of the
metropolis. In the City itself bankers and merchants played

Bristol, second largest city in England

Charles II hammered silver sixpence

James II silver halfcrown

Charles II copper farthing

Queen Anne silver shilling

William and Mary silver crown

iron-bound chest for keeping town records and treasure

coffee-house 1705

their money games. Around the wharves were dockers, sailors and boat-builders. There were timber yards, soap-works, breweries and coopers' yards, foundries and tanneries. In the coffee-houses men met to discuss the latest news or to read the newspapers: *London Gazette* (1666) official organ of the government, or *Daily Courant* (1702), *Tatler* (1709) or *Spectator* (1711). At night London was the haunt of thieves and footpads.

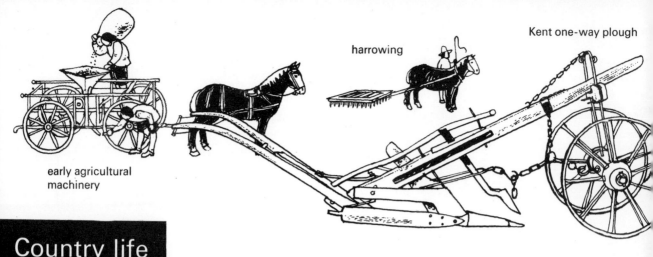

early agricultural
machinery

harrowing

Kent one-way plough

Country life

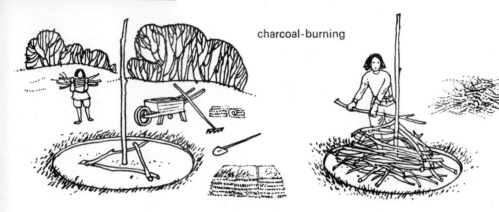

charcoal-burning

A circular area of ground was stripped of turf
and a pole set up in the centre, round which the
wood to be charked was arranged.

The stack was built up to a height of
at least 8 ft. Straw or fern, topped by
a layer of turf, was placed on the
outside.

Charcoal was dropped down the
central hole to fire the stack, and v
holes were made in the turf. Burni
lasted 5 or 6 days, followed by 3
days' cooling off.

cornfield in East Anglia

Landowners reigned like princes over their great estates.
Their magnificent mansions were set in great parks and
were filled with treasures : furniture, painting, jewellery,
gold and silver ware. Hundreds of servants, paid

beggarly wages, scurried to do the bidding of their
masters. Smaller landowners, the squires and yeomen,
suffered from heavy taxation. The poor had no share in
the prosperity of the merchants. Labourers' wages

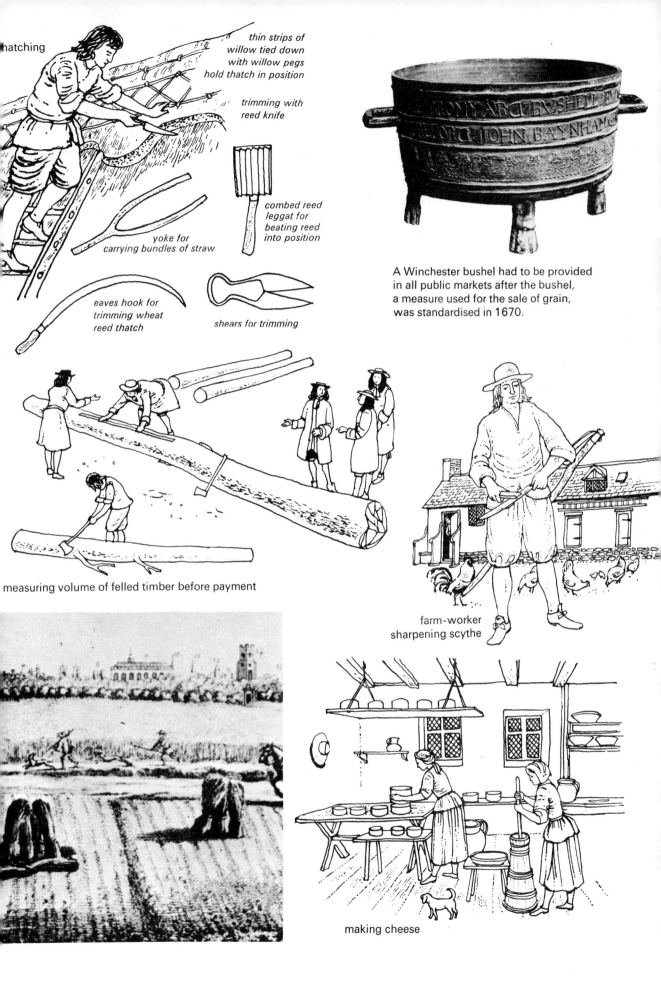

thatching

thin strips of
willow tied down
with willow pegs
hold thatch in position

trimming with
reed knife

combed reed
leggat for
beating reed
into position

yoke for
carrying bundles of straw

eaves hook for
trimming wheat
reed thatch

shears for trimming

A Winchester bushel had to be provided
in all public markets after the bushel,
a measure used for the sale of grain,
was standardised in 1670.

measuring volume of felled timber before payment

farm-worker
sharpening scythe

making cheese

remained steady while prices soared. Justices of the
Peace were supposed to fix minimum wages, but too
often neglected their duty. Skilled craftsmen could still
demand a high wage, but over-production of textiles kept

down the wages of the ordinary workmen. This affected
the weavers in the villages where most of the weaving
was still done. Agricultural labourers were the worst off.
Their living conditions were not much better than those

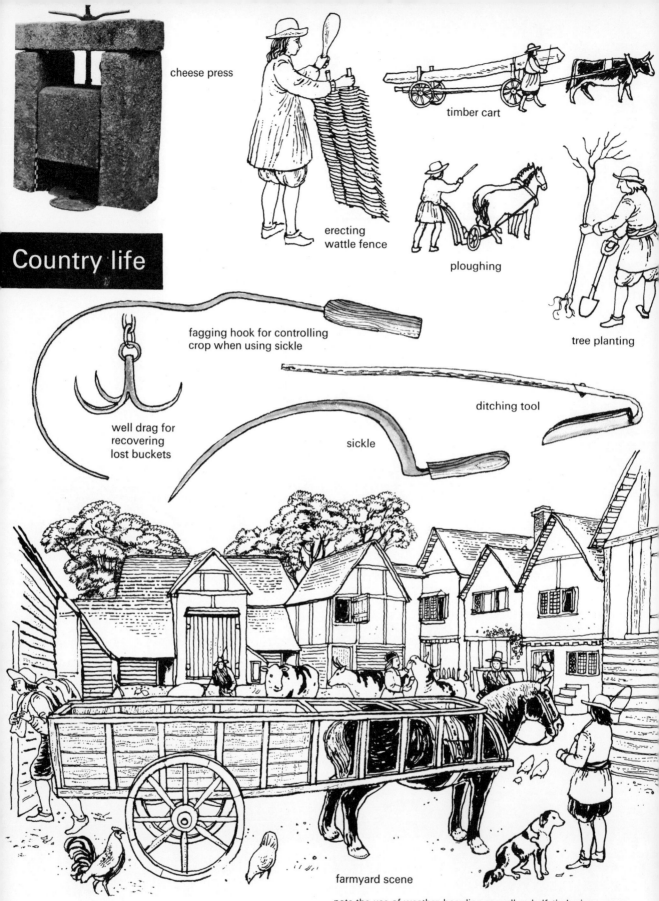

cheese press

timber cart

erecting wattle fence

ploughing

tree planting

fagging hook for controlling crop when using sickle

ditching tool

well drag for recovering lost buckets

sickle

Country life

farmyard scene

note the use of weather-boarding as well as half-timbering; a man doctoring a cow; a mounting stone; hay cart, with the load extending over the horse's back

of the animals they tended. Many still had grazing rights for their cattle despite enclosure acts. The lot of the very poor was eased by the many charitable foundations which were established during this period. The poor clergy were helped in Queen Anne's time by the surrender by the queen of the First Fruits and Tenths. This became known as 'Queen Anne's Bounty'. Much of the best farmland was still cultivated on the open-field system.

schoolmistress
and pupils

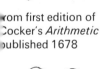
ducation

us COCKER! (Now to Reft thou'rt Gone
can Show thee fully but thine own
re Arithmetick alone can show
Sums of Thanks wee for thy Labours
owe

rom first edition of
Cocker's *Arithmetic*
published 1678

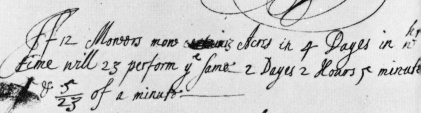

arithmetic problems in exercise book,
demonstrating 'The Rule Inverse' which would
now be called 'indirect proportion'

free school at Appleby Magna,
Leicestershire
founded by Sir John Moore, former
Lord Mayor of London;
built 1693–7

charity school
children

head of page of copybook

Cambridge and Oxford, the major universities, still confined their studies to the classics and theology. Rich landowners and merchants provided endowments to establish grammar schools. Those people who were sufficiently wealthy employed tutors. The Society for Promoting Christian Knowledge was founded in 1698 and set about establishing schools for the poor. The Nonconformists set up academies in the cities.

walnut daybed

sleeping chair
1670

Chinese 'famille noire'
vase of K'ang-hsi period
(1662–1722)

Reception rooms

English japanned cabinet on stand
of carved and silvered pinewood;
end of 17th century

ink-well with
tinderbox
late 17th
century

adjustable
socket

ink-well

sulphur
matches

pounce-box
containing
French chalk

tinder pistol

Cromwell, the Puritan, hated any display of luxury. Following his lead, furniture became plain. Carvings were banned. The Dutch influence showed itself in ball feet to the legs of tables and chairs. King Charles II

brought from the Continent some of the various styles he had seen there during his exile. Craftsmen employed by his court developed these styles in Britain. Restoration furniture had straight lines and sharp angles. Low chairs,

rushlight holder
with ratchet
for raising
or lowering

drawing-room
Ham House, Surrey, 1670s

lliam III long-case
ck made by
omas Tompion 1699
oes for 3 months and
a perpetual calendar
ich makes allowances
Leap Year

carved
beechwood
chair
about 1690

walnut
gate-legged table
1660

k bookcase made for Samuel Pepys

walnut armchair
with caned seat and back;
about 1665

Staffordshire
slipware dish

and high chairs with carved backs were a feature. Grinling Gibbons, a wood carver, created the decorations for Windsor Castle. The Dutch cabinet-makers who came with King William used marquetry. Walnut took the place

of oak. Queen Anne furniture had little ornament, but depended for its beauty upon the grace and beauty of its lines.

17th century kitchen
with meat roasting on spits,
soup in cauldron over fire,
pastry being made

wrought-iron pot hanger
4ft 8½ ins long

red stoneware teapot

oak spoon rack,
with box for knives
and forks beneath.

Pewter spoons were soft
and soon damaged
if kept in a drawer

leather beer jugs (bombards) and
drinking mugs (black jacks)

wrought-iron lock an
late 17th century

Kitchens and meals

In most homes kitchen utensils were solid, heavy and utilitarian. Jugs and mugs were made of leather or pewter. Meat roasted on spits, cauldrons hung over open fires. But the increase in trade with the Orient with the growing fashion of drinking tea, coffee and chocolate made fine china porcelain popular. Dining tables, formerly narrow, became wider to accommodate a double row of diners.

98

bed curtain of cotton and linen twill embroidered with wool

edrooms

state bed at Knole Park, Kent, 1670s
hung with cloth of gold lined with coral taffeta

silver-mounted fire irons

brass curfew
used to cover wood embers at night to keep the fire burning a little

scissors case

ut chest of drawers ; late 17th century

travelling clock by Thomas Tompion c. 1700

servants putting linen into closet

Daybeds and chests on stands were introduced in the Restoration period. Beds themselves were very elaborate, and often more magnificent than they were clean or comfortable. In Queen Mary's time they were canopied and curtained with velvet. Sometimes the canopies were decorated with plumes of feathers. The use of fabrics such as chintz and Indian embroidery became a fashion in the Queen Anne period.

seller of patches
some ladies wore black patches in different designs on their faces to emphasize their beauty

Costume

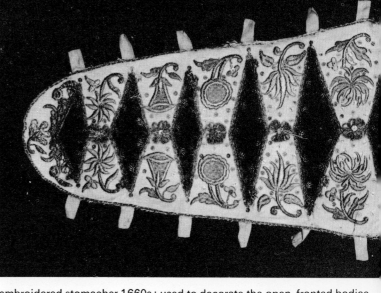

embroidered stomacher 1660s ; used to decorate the open-fronted bodice

1660–70 day gown with sleeves set low off the shoulders

This hair style was fashionable

Charles II and Queen Catherine 1662 the king wears petticoat breeches he made fashionable at Court during 1660s and '70s

Puritan dress was made of untrimmed plain material in drab colours. Men expressed their delight in the Restoration in a display of exaggerated fashion. Fussy petticoat breeches were worn with little jackets and as many yards of silk ribbon as possible. The breeches became narrower, and were then called culottes. Wigs, often called periwigs, were worn, partly to cover the clean-shaven skull of the Puritan. Waistcoats grew in

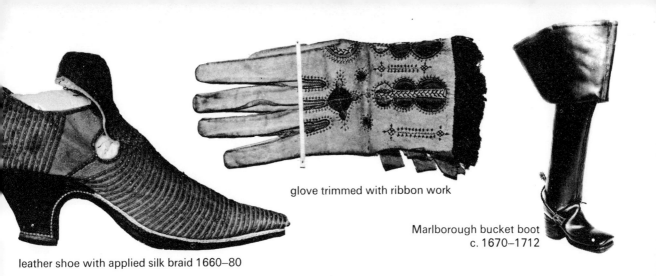

leather shoe with applied silk braid 1660–80

glove trimmed with ribbon work

Marlborough bucket boot
c. 1670–1712

gentleman (with fashionable hat of 1665–75 and long French wig) and groom

youth in puritanical clothes 1676

brother and sister 1695

boy dressed like a girl before being 'breeched' which usually took place about the age of seven

man wearing periwig 1690

popularity. Faces were clean-shaven. Women wore low-cut bodices. Hoods were worn out-of-doors over hair wired to make the curls stand out. Indoors the fontange, a tall headdress, was sometimes worn. The bodice was sewn on to a skirt with a long train. But women liked to appear tiny-waisted and wore tight peaked bodices with steel busks or corsets underneath. Underskirts were trimmed with frills and flounces.

the Seven Bishops on the way to The
Tower at the command of James II, 1688
They had petitioned against his decree that
the Declaration of Indulgence should be
read by the clergy in all churches

King

Dr Oates discovereth ȳ Plot
to ȳ King and Councell

War, politics and government

Battle of Oudenarde 1708
in the War of the Spanish Succession

playing-card showing
Titus Oates
who in 1678 claimed to
have discovered a Papist
plot to murder Charles

James, Duke of Monmouth,
tried to seize the crown
from James II in 1685,
and was executed on
Tower Hill on 15 July

John Churchill,
1st Duke of
Marlborough
1650-1722
English general
and politician

Throughout most of the period there were wars at sea and
on land. There were three wars against the Dutch,
challenging their supremacy. Admiral Robert Blake
defeated Tromp, but the Dutch admiral Ruyter sailed up

the Thames and caused havoc with the British fleet.
Later there were major successes for British armies on the
Continent. In the War of the Spanish Succession, the
Duke of Marlborough won a series of battles including

The Tichborne Dole (1670) ; painting by Gillis van Tilborch
villagers await the distribution of the hereditary charity by
Henry Tichborne, who stands in front of his Tudor house
rounded by family and servants. This ceremony survives today

The Oxford election
from a painting by Egbert van Heenskerck 1687

1685 coronation
procession of
James II,
formerly Lord
High Admiral

Samuel Pepys
was one of his
canopy-bearers

Ramillies and Blenheim. At home throughout the Stuart period the country was bedevilled with religious problems. With William and Mary the country settled for Protestantism. There was a decline in fanaticism in politics and of intolerance in religion. Superstition declined ; the last occasion an English court convicted a woman of witchcraft was in 1712. Monarchy predominated less in politics and the Whigs and Tories struggled for power.

crowds fleeing from London during the plague of 1665

Plague and medicine

blood-letting was a favourite remedy for illness

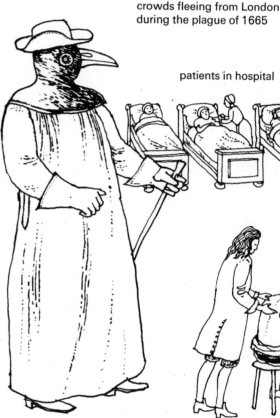

costume worn by doctors visiting those stricken by plague

The beak was stuffed with perfumes

patients in hospital

cupping and bleeding

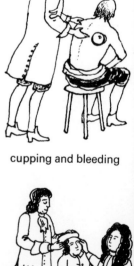

court oculist Sir William Read treating a patient

mouth-feeler

proboscis for piercing and sucking

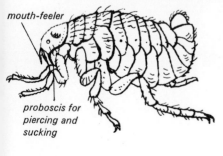

flea, only about 1mm in length

black rat, usually about 17 ins long including tail

Bubonic fever is spread by fleas on black rats. This was not known when the fever, called the Great Plague, came to London in 1665. It spread rapidly through the tightly-packed houses. In May 43 people died of the plague; in September 30,000 died. Doctors fled with other citizens except for a few brave men who attempted to help the suffering.

Landmarks in civilization, 1661 to 1714

1661 Robert Boyle, the Irish chemist and physicist, published *The Sceptical Chemist*, the first attempt at defining chemical elements.
Louis XIV of France began building the Palace of Versailles.
The Bank of Sweden, founded in 1656, printed the first paper banknotes.
Ruisdael, Dutch landscape painter, painted *Landscape with Watermill.*

1662 Sir Christopher Wren designed the Sheldonian Theatre, Oxford.
Revised version of the Prayer Book issued.
Boyle described his famous law of the expansion of gases.

1664 Robert Hooke, an English experimental scientist, published *Micrographia.*

1665 Bernini, Italian sculptor, completed High Altar of St Peter's Church in Rome with his famous bronze canopy.
Hooke announced his discovery that plants breathe.

1666 Great Fire of London destroyed a great part of the city, leading to Sir Christopher Wren's rebuilding programme.
Molière's *Le Misanthrope* produced.
London Gazette established as the official government journal.
Marcello Malpighi, Italian anatomist, described red corpuscles in his book *Anatomical Treatise on the Structures of the Viscera.*

1667 John Milton wrote his epic poem *Paradise Lost.*

1670 Hudson Bay Trading Company founded to trade in Canada.
Pascal's *Pensées*, his philosophical thoughts on religion, published posthumously.

1671 Malpighi published work on plant tissues.
Wren, who designed more than 50 churches after the Great Fire, began to build the Monument to commemorate the Great Fire.

1672 Vanderheide invented flexible fire hose.

1673 Jean Racine, famous French playwright, wrote *Mithridate*, one of his seven masterpieces.

1675 Wycherley, famous for his comedies of manners, wrote his best-known play, *The Country Wife.*
Baruch Spinoza, Dutch philosopher, completed his great work, *Ethics.*
Anton van Leeuwenhoek, the Dutch scientist, discovered protozoa with his microscope and described red blood corpuscles.
Olaus Roemer, Danish astronomer, used calculations based on Jupiter to estimate the speed of light, which he assessed at about 192,000 miles a second.
Huyghens made balance-wheel for watches.
Royal Observatory built at Greenwich with John Flamsteed appointed first Astronomer Royal.

1676 Edmund Halley published star catalogue of the southern sky, result of telescopic observation on St Helena.

1677 Halley observed transit of Venus.

1678 John Bunyan's *The Pilgrim's Progress* published: religious allegory written in jail.
Hooke stated his theory of elasticity in *Hooke's Law*: the amount an elastic body stretches out of shape is in direct proportion to the force acting upon it.

1679 Purcell, the English composer, became organist at Westminster Abbey.
Denis Papin, French physicist, invented the 'steam digester' that ultimately led to the steam engine.

1680 Andrew Marvell's poems published: a metaphysical poet who supported Cromwell but wrote about non-religious subjects.

1681 Thomas Burnet wrote *Sacred Theory of the Earth* which contained an imaginative description of the evolution of the earth.
William Penn, the Quaker, granted patent for setting up a colony in America, from which came Pennsylvania.
La Salle, French explorer, travelled the Mississippi and claimed the surrounding territory for France: later called Louisiana.

1682 Halley's comet observed, proving the astronomer's theory.
Otway's *Venice Preserved* produced.

1683 William Dockwra instituted London penny postal service.
Leeuwenhoek made sketches of the bacteria observed through his microscope.

1684 Robert Hooke invented the heliograph: instrument used to send messages by reflected sunlight from mirrors.
Bermuda became Crown Colony.
Dryden's poems published.

1685 William Dampier, exploring in the South Seas, reached New Holland (Australia).
Newton discovered gravitational theories.

1687 Newton's great work *Philosophiae Naturalis Principia Mathematica* published: provided basis for modern mathematics.
Talman began building Chatsworth, home of the Dukes of Devonshire.
Grand Trianon erected in Versailles.

1688 Dampier explored coast of Australia.

1689 Purcell's opera *Dido and Aeneas* produced: first English opera.

1690 John Locke, English philosopher, expressed his political philosophy in *Two Treatises of Government.*
Borrow's Worcester Journal, first weekly provincial newspaper, was published as the *Worcester Postman.*
Christian Huyghens, Dutch physicist and astronomer, published *Traité de la Lumière*, a study of light.

1691 Surveyors of Highways appointed for each parish to see that roads were maintained.

1692 Purcell's song 'Nymphs and Shepherds' published in *The Libertine.*
Edward Lloyd's coffee-house established as headquarters for marine insurance.

1694 Bank of England established by William Paterson and developed by him with help from the government.
Chelsea Royal Hospital for soldiers opened.

1695 Bishop Ken wrote the hymn 'Awake, my Soul'.

1696 Sir John Vanbrugh, architect and playwright, wrote *The Relapse,* a comedy.
John Aubrey, the antiquarian, who first discovered the origin of Stonehenge, published his *Miscellanies.*
First Eddystone lighthouse built by Henry Winstanley.

1696 Jacob Bernoulli developed the theory of probability and the calculus of variations at the University of Basel in Switzerland.
Academy of Arts founded at Berlin.

1697 Charles Perrault published a collection of fairy tales under his son's name: *Contes du Temps Passé*.
Silver articles required to be manufactured at Britannia standard.
Grinling Gibbons carved stalls in St Paul's Cathedral.

1698 Foundation of SPCK (Society for Promoting Christian Knowledge).
Newton calculated speed of sound.
Thomas Savery patented first practical steam engine.

1699 Billingsgate Market became London's chief fish market.
Dampier sailed to Australia in the *Roebuck*.

1700 Congreve's *The Way of the World* produced.
Peter the Great carrying out reforms in Russia.

1701 *Hankampu*, a famous Japanese history by Hakuseki, published.
Jethro Tull invented seed drill for multiple sowing.

1702 *Daily Courant*, London's first daily newspaper, published.

1703 Peter the Great founded St Petersburg, now Leningrad.
First Russian newspaper, *Vyedomosti*, published.

1704 Jonathan Swift wrote *A Tale of a Tub*.
Newton's *Opticks* published describing his theory of light.
Leibnitz, German mathematician and philosopher, published *Nouveaux Essais sur l'Entendement humain*.

1705 Vanbrugh began the building of Blenheim Palace presented by the nation to John Churchill, Duke of Marlborough.
Ship's wheel used for the first time to replace the tiller.

1706 Farquhar wrote *The Beaux' Stratagem*.
L'Hôtel des Invalides built in Paris.

1707 Isaac Watts' hymns published.

1709 Johann Böttger discovered secrets of Chinese porcelain and produced Dresden china.
Johann Farina produced eau-de-cologne.
Abraham Darby used coke to smelt iron.
Bartolomeo Cristofori worked out principle of striking hammer against string to make a keyboard instrument that he called *gravicembalo col piano e forte:* the beginning of the pianoforte.

1710 Sir Christopher Wren completed St Paul's Cathedral.
First English Copyright Act came into force.

1711 Joseph Addison founded *The Spectator*, introducing Sir Roger de Coverley.
Academy of Arts established in London by Sir Godfrey Kneller.
Newcomen, a blacksmith, constructed practical steam engine.

1712 Alexander Pope wrote *The Rape of the Lock*, a satirical poem.
Last execution in England for witchcraft.

1713 Peter the Great founded naval harbour at Tallinn.
Proof of binomial theorem established in Bernouilli's *De Arte conjectandi*.

1714 Gabriel Fahrenheit, a German physicist, introduced thermometer with the temperature scale named after him.
Handel composed his *Water Music*.

Georgians

Research, design and illustration
by B. S. Biro, FSIA

*THE GEORGIAN PERIOD extends from 1714 when, upon
the death of Queen Anne, George, the Elector of Hanover,
succeeded to the British throne. It ends with the accession
of Queen Victoria. It was the period of great prosperity, and
yet in these years the industrial slums were created. Some
of our greatest literature and finest music were composed
in this period. Yet people enjoyed public executions and
cock-fighting. Fortunately, Britain avoided the bloodstained
horror of revolution, such as the French suffered, and had
the satisfaction of finally dispersing the shadow of Napoleon
over Europe. The burgeoning of the British Empire in the
Victorian period had yet to come.*

George I   George II   George III

George IV   William IV

Leicester cornfields, still unenclosed in 1743;
a contemporary engraving

Farming

winnowing fan,
separating grain
from chaff

Robert Bakewell

agricultural labou

swingle of a flail

Jethro Tull's plough
and wheat drill

cowherd and milkmaid; painting by Morland

The rapid change in farming methods begun by
enclosures of common land caused poverty and distress
to the villagers. But farmers had to meet the greater
demand caused by the rapid increase in population. With

enclosures, farmers improved their arable land. Cattle
could be bred to give more milk and provide better meat.
Men like Coke, Townshend, Bakewell and Tull led the
way. Thomas Coke and 'Turnip' Townshend experi-

as Coke inspecting his Southdown sheep at Holkham;
ving by William Ward from painting by Thomas Weaver 1808

an eighteenth-century farm

reaping

harvest home 1813

a farmer and his wife

mented with a rotation of crops. They grew root crops
(hence Townshend's nickname) to feed livestock. Coke
grew wheat instead of rye and improved breeds of
cattle, sheep and pigs. Robert Bakewell of Leicestershire
developed in-breeding to improve the best features in
cattle and sheep. Jethro Tull of Berkshire invented a drill
for boring straight rows of holes into which the seed
was dropped.

collier loading a wagon 1788

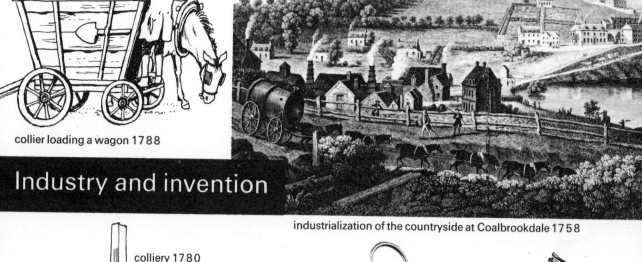

Industry and invention

industrialization of the countryside at Coalbrookdale 1758

colliery 1780

Davy safety lamp
used in mines

weaving

mill

iron works

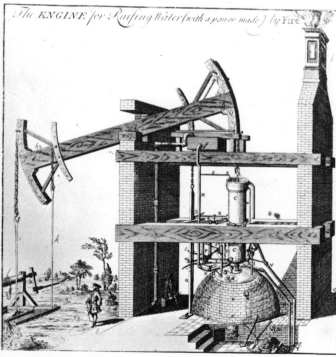

Newcomen's steam engine 1712

Since the dawn of history, man had used his muscle and brawn, and the muscle and brawn of his domesticated animals, to wrest a living from the earth. The wheel, the plough, the spinning wheel and the loom were the limits of his inventive genius. But, in the eighteenth century, man discovered the use of machinery. James Watt's steam engine provided another source of power to the windmill and water-wheel. Lancashire inventors improved

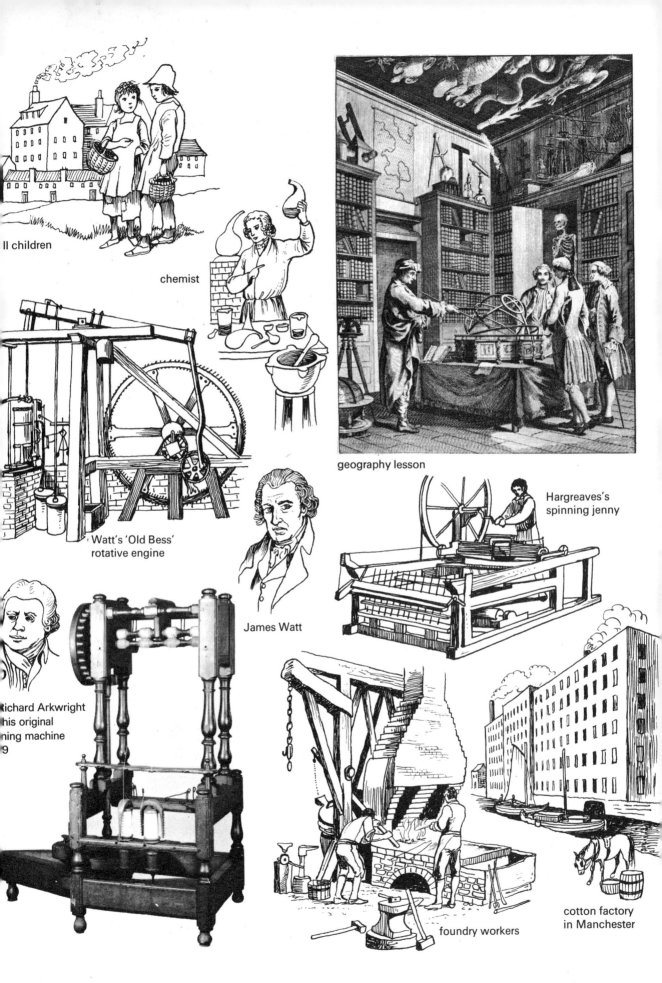

ll children

chemist

geography lesson

Watt's 'Old Bess' rotative engine

James Watt

Hargreaves's spinning jenny

Richard Arkwright
his original
ning machine
9

foundry workers

cotton factory
in Manchester

textile manufacture with multiple spinning machines.
Arkwright opened cotton mills that combined manu-
facturing processes in one factory. Seeking the greater
prosperity of the machine age, men flocked to the

coal-mining valleys and the new factory towns. Here,
in confined and unhygienic conditions, men, women,
and even children, worked long hours for little pay.

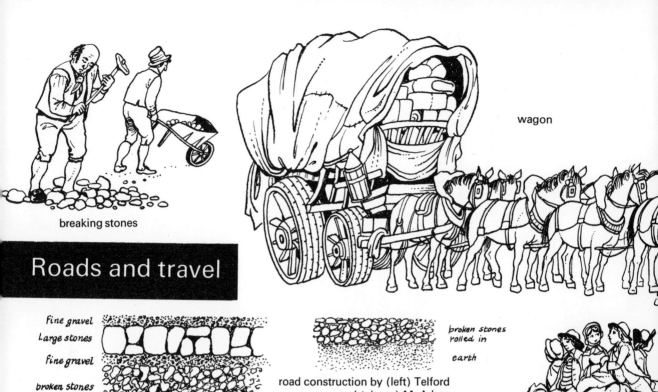

breaking stones

Roads and travel

wagon

Fine gravel
Large stones
Fine gravel

broken stones

broken stones
rolled in

earth

road construction by (left) Telford
and (above) McAdam

first iron bridge
at Coalbrookdale 1779

stage-coach at a turnpike

'Country Inn Courtyard'
by Hogarth

sedan chair

The growth of industrial towns increased road traffic enormously. The narrow badly-surfaced lanes and roads that linked villages and market towns soon became inadequate. New roads were built by parishes and turnpike trusts, paid for by tolls collected from travellers. The first practical road engineer in Britain was 'Blind Jack' Metcalf of Knaresborough. Other road builders were Thomas Telford, who also constructed some

...tail of George III's ...ate coach 1762

'The Overset' by Rowlandson

Reproduced by gracious permission of Her Majesty Queen Elizabeth II

...ndau

gig

post-chaise

perch phaeton

Lunardi's balloon 1784

...ick's *Catch-me-who-can,* London 1808

highwayman

wonderful bridges, and John Loudon McAdam, who introduced a new method of road construction. Despite the constant threat of attack by highwaymen and footpads, the roads became busy thoroughfares. But within a few years Richard Trevithick had invented his locomotive. Some men were even looking to the air for faster methods of travel.

from Gilbert White's *Natural History of Selborne* 1789

Village life

village parson

milkmaid

wheelwright

smithy

pedlar

cottage industry

villagers; by Bewick

The enclosure of the common lands meant a reconstitution of village life. The rich farmers became richer and extended their enclosures. The smallholders lost their independence with their land. They worked for the big farmers. Factory towns made home crafts unprofitable. Village weavers took out-work from the factories. Villagers worked hard, wore hand-woven clothes and kept a cow or a pig.

on the sands at Worthing; by Nixon 1808

Watering places

bathing machine 1791

Sayer's Machine

pump room of the King's Bath at Bath 1789

bath chair on North Parade, Bath 1777

Brummell

MONTPELLIER SPA

arrival of the Margate hoy

morning promenade at Cheltenham; by Cruikshank

The ancient Roman baths became popular again, and Bath was the most fashionable town in England. Wealthy people with time on their hands spent it in the delights of The Season, so ably conducted by Beau Nash and Beau Brummell. Balls were gay and dignified occasions; gambling was an obsession. Brighton and Scarborough were the popular seaside resorts for the 'quality'. Ordinary folk went to Margate.

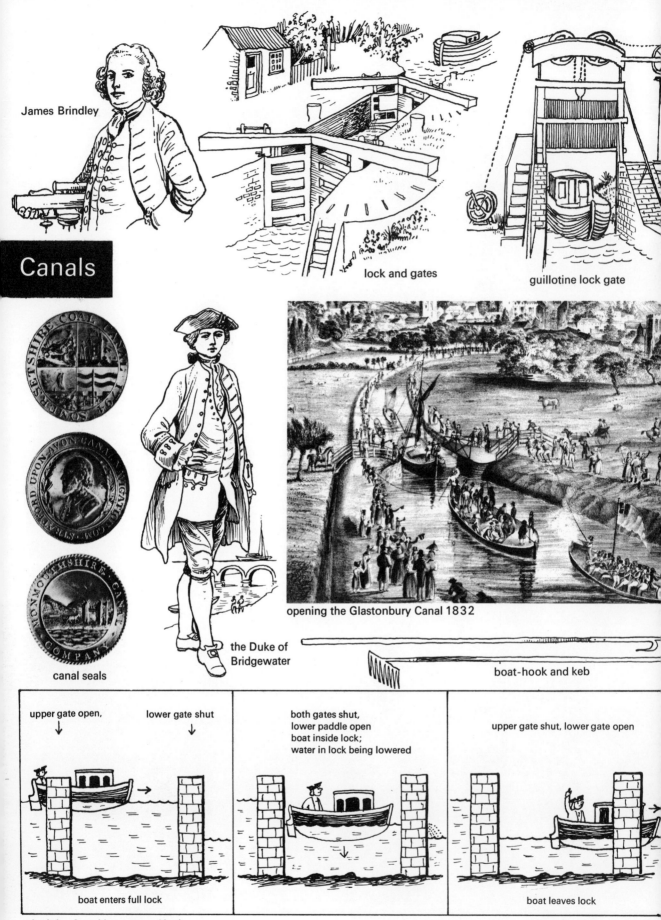

James Brindley

lock and gates

guillotine lock gate

canal seals

the Duke of Bridgewater

opening the Glastonbury Canal 1832

boat-hook and keb

upper gate open,
↓

lower gate shut
↓

boat enters full lock

both gates shut,
lower paddle open
boat inside lock;
water in lock being lowered

upper gate shut, lower gate open

boat leaves lock

principle of working a pound lock

The first canals in Britain were built to transport coal cheaply from the mines to the factory towns. James Brindley built for the Duke of Bridgewater a canal between his mines and Manchester. This reduced the price of the coal by half, and brought in 80 years of canal-building fever. During this time more than 4,000 miles of navigable waterways were constructed. The most noted engineers were James Brindley, William

Barton Aqueduct across the river Irwell

legging through Shrewley Tunnel

the *Charlotte Dundas,*
the first canal steamboat 1801

opening the paddles
of a lock

canal seal

barges at the sluice gate

orridge Canal and Rolle Aqueduct, Devon 1823

Jessop, Thomas Telford, John Rennie, Benjamin Outram and Thomas Dadford. Gangs of navigators, who became known as navvies, provided the labour. They worked with spade and shovel, wagon and wheelbarrow.

The first canals followed the contours of the land. Later, engineers became more ambitious. Embankments and cuttings maintained levels. Aqueducts and tunnels were built, and locks were common features of the rural landscape.

Captain Coram,
founder of the Foundling Hospital

press gang from 'The Liberty of the Subject' by Gi

Ills of man

beating hemp in prison

Newgate prison

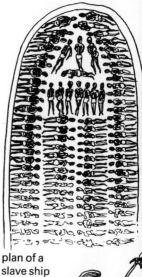

plan of a
slave ship

tumbril

scene in a madhouse from Hogarth's 'Rake's Progress'

The Industrial Revolution brought poverty, squalor and anguish to many people. They tried to drown their sorrows in gin, which was an inexpensive drink. Badly paid and half-starved, poor people in the towns stole.

Peasants poached. Punishment was severe. A man could be hanged for stealing a sheep and transported for taking a loaf. Hogarth satirized the vice and cruelty of his age. Prisoners were treated inhumanly and

ward in Guy's Hospital

'humane' man-trap

treadmill

Edward Jenner vaccinating against smallpox

surgical instruments

'Gin Lane' by Hogarth

communal grave

executions were a public spectacle. Press-gangs, forcing wayfarers into the navy, were kept busy. Lack of sanitation and open drains in towns brought persistent fevers. Hospitals were crowded and nurses untrained.

Surgery without anaesthetic was agony for doctor and patient. In 1776, however, Jenner's use of vaccination had challenged endemic smallpox, a dread disease.

oyster-seller

Great Piazza, Covent Garden

street musicians by Hogarth

buying wallpaper

fish porter at Billingsgate

view of the City from Somerset House by Canaletto *Reproduced by gracious permission of Her Majesty Queen Elizabeth II*

London

After the Great Fire in 1666, Sir Christopher Wren planned a new and beautiful London. But his plans were discarded. However, he rebuilt St Paul's and many other London churches. He also built the Royal Observatory at Greenwich. Wood was banned in the rebuilding of London, but the streets were kept narrow and there were open drains. London's importance grew with the growing prosperity of industrial Britain. The Bank of England

view of Westminster Bridge by Canaletto
Reproduced by gracious permission of Her Majesty Queen Elizabeth II

a coffee house

Bow
Street
runner

Johnson and James Boswell;
er Rowlandson

gingerbread man

St George's,
Hanover Square

attracted trade to the City. The Stock Exchange was founded in 1773. From one of the many popular coffee house meeting places grew the great shipping insurance firm of Lloyd's. The partnership of shipping, banking and insurance increased the wealth and international importance of the metropolis. Markets and elegant shops met the needs of a population that reached one million in 1800.

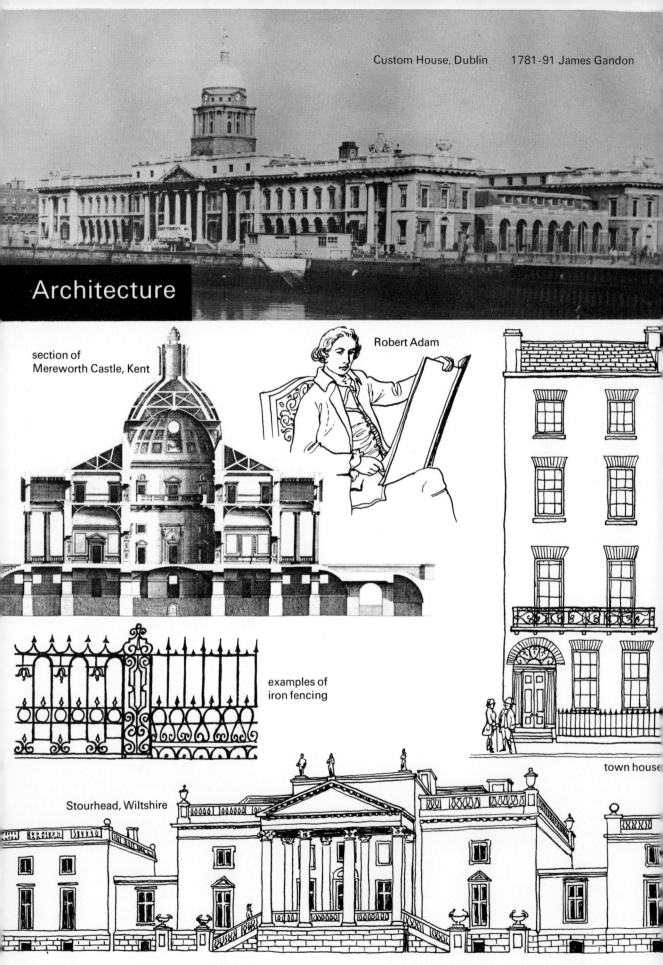

Architecture

section of
Mereworth Castle, Kent

Robert Adam

examples of
iron fencing

town house

Stourhead, Wiltshire

From 1725 architects forsook the elaborate Stuart style of architecture and developed a formal style known as Anglo-Palladianism. Andrea Palladio was an Italian architect whose work inspired Inigo Jones. Anglo-

Palladian architecture gradually gained the classical grace of the Georgian style, which became one of the most gracious periods in the history of architecture. The Earl of Burlington led the movement. Stately

Fonthill Abbey; engraving showing west and north fronts

gateway of Burlington House 1716

Theatre Royal,
Drury Lane

doorway 1750

cottages in
a country town

St Mary-le-Strand, London; engraving by Maurer 1753

country mansions were built by Colin Campbell, William Kent and Sir Edward L. Pearce in landscaped gardens. Formal terraces and squares maintained the classic style in London, Bath and Dublin. The skills of Robert Adam and James Wyatt brought in the elegance of the Regency style.

William Kent

'Capability' Brown

mid-eighteenth century bridge at Stowe

Gardens

garden gates at Ince Blundell Hall, Lancashire

gatepost finial

garden temple

pagoda fountain at Alton Towers

Clumber Park, Nottinghamshire

'ruins' at Kew

William Kent and his pupil, Lancelot 'Capability' Brown, were the first to introduce 'landscape' gardening. They aimed to create natural effects by artificial means. Brown acquired his nickname from his habit of claiming to see 'capabilities' in grounds he was asked to landscape. Rolling fields with clumps of trees were given additional features of temples, bridges and decorated 'ruins', known as follies.

licking the raw recruit
into shape 1780

bayonet c.1750

sword 1742

Brown Bess
musket 1717

pistol 1745

powder horn

the army

shako
1816

...oon 1815

Regiment of
Foot 1770

general
1785

Royal English Fusilier 1742

hussar 1809

...e of Waterloo

Britain was forced to maintain a large army. The ranks were manned by some of the roughest men in the land. Yet they showed indomitable courage in the face of danger. In drawn-out campaigns such as the Peninsular War they displayed great stamina and endurance, and in the victories of Quebec, Plassey and Waterloo the British Army demonstrated its qualities as a fine fighting force.

magnetic dry-card
ship's compass 1750

Ships

THE SECTION OF A FIRST RATE SHIP

A-Fore.   The Midships.   A-Baft.

The-Fore-Maft.   Main-Maft.   Mifon-Maft.

seamen 1795

Captain Cook's
Endeavour

naval cannon and chain shot

captain
1760

stern of the *Royal George* (model) 1756

HMS *Centurion*, 60 guns, 1732,
in which Anson later sailed round the world

This was the second great period in British naval history.
Increased commerce established a great merchant fleet
which traded with the world, despite the piracy that
flourished on the high seas. Life on board was hard and
cruel. Men were away from home for many months at a
time. Sailors went without fresh food for long periods.
Until lime water was discovered to be a preventative,
scurvy was rife. Sailing ships were at the mercy of storms.

ress-gang

d the navy

sailor heaving the lead 1807

Horatio,
Viscount Nelson

HMS *Victory*, 100 guns;
Nelson's flagship at Trafalgar 1805

quadrant and telescope

anchor

officer's button

stern
lanthorn

battle 1794

It was not surprising that manpower had to be recruited by the notorious press-gangs, and that crews often mutinied. Yet, during this period Cook explored the South Seas. Anson sailed round the world in the H.M.S. *Centurion*.

Nelson achieved a succession of naval victories that confined Napoleon's domination to the Continent. Trafalgar was the last battle when fleets of warships with sails fought in formation on the open seas.

Chippendale designs for borders
for paper hangings

Interiors

lamp stand

carved oak staircase
by William Kent

doorcase in the Chinese Room,
Claydon House 1760

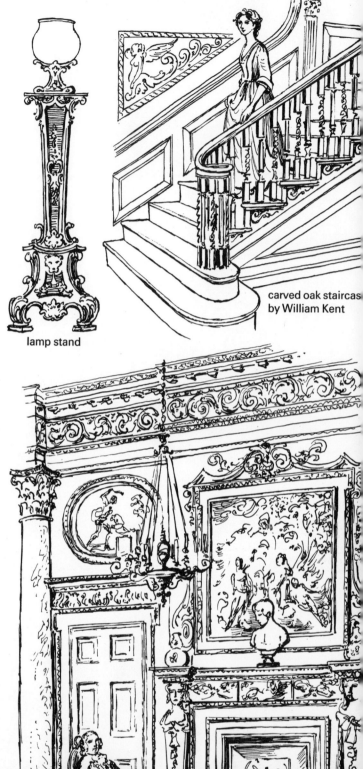

early Georgian stucco at Stoneleigh Abbey

In the first half of the eighteenth century the leading
designer in the Palladian style was William Kent, a
Yorkshire architect. In addition to work as a landscape
gardener and as a painter, William Kent designed

magnificently decorated ceilings, and exquisite door-
ways and chimney-pieces. Gilt furniture showed up
against this splendour. In the tall and dignified rooms of
country mansions and town houses, often decorated

carved candle
stand 1730

in a shepherd's cottage 1788

washstand 1760

country house kitchen 1800

bedroom with fourposter bed

library at Kenwood by Robert Adam 1767

with plaster work and carving, every detail combined
to produce an elegant, harmonious whole. Adam is the
great name in interior decoration. The Adams were four
Scottish brothers who all trained as architects. Robert

Adam replaced the Palladian style with a distinctive
classical design which became famous as Adam style.
This style covered all aspects of architecture and interior
decoration.

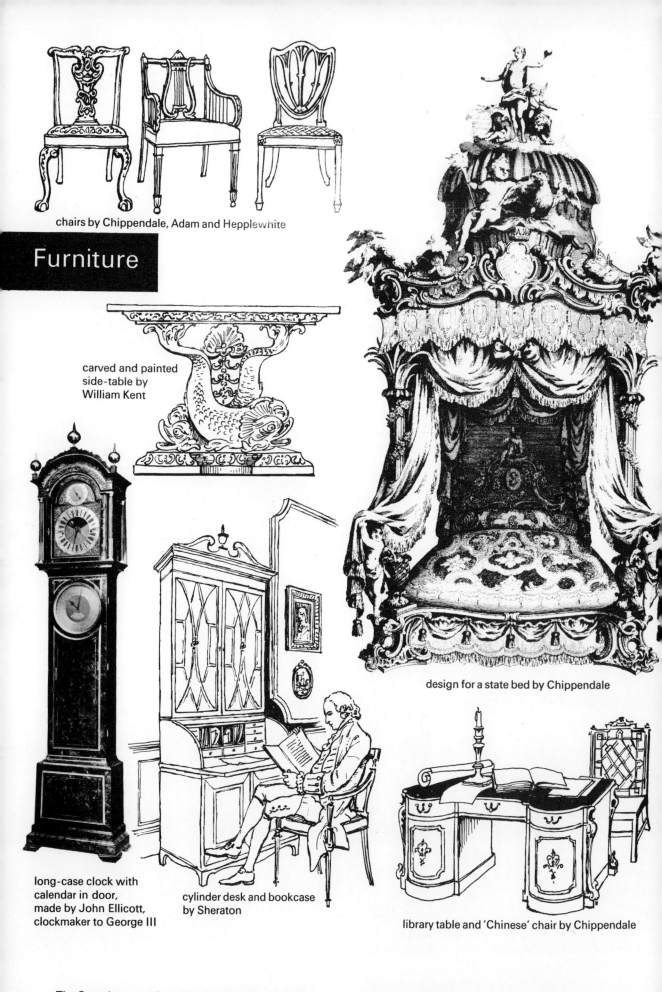

chairs by Chippendale, Adam and Hepplewhite

Furniture

carved and painted side-table by William Kent

design for a state bed by Chippendale

long-case clock with calendar in door, made by John Ellicott, clockmaker to George III

cylinder desk and bookcase by Sheraton

library table and 'Chinese' chair by Chippendale

The Georgians saw the greatest achievements of the cabinet-maker's art. Furniture was ideally functional, perfect in proportion and beautiful in detail. Chippendale (1718?-1779) borrowed freely from Gothic, French and Chinese designs, but developed his own style. The arts of marquetry and lacquer in the Chinese style were perfected in the work of Hepplewhite. Sheraton used rectangular shapes, and straight-lined inlay and carving.

yellow glass bowl c.1825 Irish

gilded wood girandole 1750

ecorative arts

Chelsea porcelain 1745

soup tureen 1746

steel and brass basket grate 1780

pinewood chimney glass, carved and gilded c.1774

George I silver coffee pot and sugar dredger

jasper vase by Wedgwood 1790

Chippendale designs for brass handle and escutcheons

The discovery of making porcelain allowed craftsmen of great skill to express the Georgian spirit in the most delicate manner. Many objects of wood or metal show exquisite taste and fine workmanship. Josiah Wedgwood (1730-1779) was the outstanding ceramics manufacturer. He developed the creamware called Queen's Ware, and the fine Jasperware. The Waterford cut-glass of this period from Ireland is particularly notable.

theatre ticket designed by Hogarth

The arts

scene from 'The Clandestine Marriage'; painting by Zoffany

girl wire dancer at Sadler's Wells

country dancers; engraving by George Bickham

Mrs Siddons as 'The Tragic Muse'

Covent Garden Opera House 1809 (later burnt down)

scene from Gay's 'Beggar's Opera'; after Hogarth

lights with dimmers

woodcut of circus rider

The Age of Reason in the Arts was still flourishing when King George I came to the throne. The satirists Alexander Pope and Jonathan Swift were publishing some of their best work. Pope's 'New Dunciad' was published in 1743. *Gulliver's Travels* appeared in 1726. But by the middle of the eighteenth century the Age of Reason influence on literature had worked itself out. The Romantics brought in a new form of literature. William

George Frederick Handel

steel engraving by George Bickham

Musick

bookseller's shop

Dr Samuel Johnson

Thomas Gainsborough

A View of the Royal Exhibition at Somerset House

painter in his studio

William Hogarth by Roubiliac

Wordsworth, Samuel Taylor Coleridge and Robert Southey lived and worked in the Lake District. Famous portrait painters of the period were Sir Joshua Reynolds and Thomas Gainsborough. John Constable introduced vivid colours into his landscapes. Handel composed his oratorios, John Gay put 'The Beggar's Opera' on the stage and Thomas Arne composed 'Rule, Britannia'.

ladies' cricket 1779

cricket 1750

Sports and pastimes

the cotillion dance 1771

trotting match

fox-hunting

the hobby-horse

skati

a country race-course 1786

Some of Britain's national sports, including cricket, became popular during this period. Prize-fights attracted crowds, and in 1719 James Figg was declared to be the first champion boxer of England. Fox-hunting was popular with the aristocracy and yeoman farmers. Cock-fighting, bull- and bear-baiting drew other sections of the public. The favourite entertainment centres in London were Ranelagh and Vauxhall Gardens.

battledore and
shuttlecock

peep-show 1808

cock-fighting; by Hogarth

Rotunda, Ranelagh Gardens

shooting and
fishing

backgammon

bull-baiting

rize-fight

Vauxhall Gardens 1765

For country people there was the annual visit of the fair, vulgar and rowdy, but hailed as an eventful change in a hard-working dreary existence. At night and during the dull winter days people enjoyed gambling, backgammon and battledore and shuttlecock (ancestor to badminton). And for glitter, dignity and elegance there was the ball, with formal manners and formal dances.

1725

1735

1755

1765

1720

styles in hats

Costume

side hoop and corset 1740

girl's cap 1725

dandy 1740

periwig 1761

in the country 1755

A Hint to the Ladies to take Care of their HEADS.

satirical·print 1776

in town 1781

fashionable hair-styles and hats 1776

Villagers wore home-spun clothes which lacked elegance but were hard-wearing and warm. Poor townspeople wore rags or cast-offs from people who were better off than they were. Men in the upper classes

as well as women were elegant in embroidered silk and velvet. Women's hairstyles varied from simple curls to the most elaborate structures. Men had powdered wigs. At social centres such as Bath and Brighton in the Regency

Hon. Mrs Graham; by Gainsborough 1776

woman's shoe 1775

1780

bonnet 1788

gentleman 1781

riding dress 1806

woman's shoe 1812

children 1787

walking costume 1818

young lady 1820

period men flaunted themselves like peacocks. Men such as Beau Brummell set the fashion. The slightest breach of etiquette or error of judgment in dress could mean a person's exile from the social circles. Eventually the tightly-laced bodices and hooped skirts gave way to flimsy, simple dresses in the 'classical' style. Men forsook the elaborate Regency styles and their clothes became simpler and duller.

upper-class children
at play 1785

listening to a story;
woodcut

Children

the schoolmistress; painting by Opie

schoolroo

working in a rope factory

horse-on-rockers
1820

cup and ball 1820

Children in rich families dressed as adults from an early age. Nurses and governesses watched over their welfare, until they were old enough to go to boarding-schools. They rode and shot and joined the hunt. Poor children had little education. They went to work when they were very young. But in 1780 Robert Raikes opened his Sunday School to teach children to read and write. This system spread throughout the country.

Landmarks in civilization, 1715 to 1837

1715 Antonio Stradivari made violins.

1717 Halley discovered true motion of fixed stars.

1719 Daniel Defoe wrote *Robinson Crusoe*.

1721 Johann Sebastian Bach composed *Brandenburg Concertos*.

1724 Three Choirs Festival, oldest British music festival, began: Gloucester, Worcester and Hereford.

1725 John Flamsteed's star catalogue published.

1726 Jonathan Swift's *Gulliver's Travels* published.

1728 Pope wrote his satire *The Dunciad*.
Gay's opera, *Beggar's Opera* produced.

1730 Viscount Townshend introduced Four-year Rotation of Crops.

1731 Hadley and Godfrey, working independently, invented navigational sextant.
L'Abbé Prévost wrote *Manon Lescaut*.
Benjamin Franklin founded free public library in Philadelphia.

1732 First Covent Garden Opera House opened.

1733 John Kay's flying shuttle shuttle loom patented.

1735 Russian Imperial Ballet School founded.
William Hogarth, satirist, drew *A Rake's Progress*.
John Harrison invented the first chronometer.
Carl Linnaeus began his plant classification.

1736 Leonhard Euler, Swiss mathematician, compiled *Mechanica:* foundation of analytical mathematics.
India-rubber introduced into Europe.

1740 Samuel Richardson wrote *Pamela*.

1742 Handel composed *The Messiah*, an oratorio.

1745 Robert Bakewell began experiments to improve sheep breeding.

1748 Richardson wrote *Clarissa Harlowe;* Tobias Smollett wrote *Roderick Random*.
Lewis Paul invented machines for wool carding.

1749 Henry Fielding wrote *Tom Jones*.

1750 Thomas Gray composed *Elegy written in a Country Churchyard*.
Clarinet was introduced into a French orchestra.

1751 First volume of *Encyclopédie* produced: a collaboration of Diderot, Rousseau, Voltaire and Montesquieu.
Cronstedt, Swedish scientist, isolated nickel.

1752 Benjamin Franklin invented the lightning conductor.
Gregorian Calendar (1582) adopted in Britain.

1754 John Canton invented the electroscope.
Henry Cort invented iron-rolling process.

1755 Dr Samuel Johnson's *Dictionary of the English Language* produced.
Euler produced *Institutiones Calculi Differentialis*, first book on differential calculus.

1756 Porcelain factory founded at Sèvres.

1759 Voltaire's *Candide* published.
James Brindley constructed Bridgewater Canal.
Britain's oldest ironworks still active (Carron Iron Works) founded.
Smeaton's Eddystone Lighthouse opened.

1760 Laurence Sterne wrote *Tristram Shandy*.
Josiah Wedgwood began producing his pottery in Etruria in Staffordshire.
Kew Botanical Gardens opened.

1764 London Literary Club founded: among members were Sir Joshua Reynolds, Dr Samuel Johnson, Oliver Goldsmith, James Boswell and Edmund Burke.

1765 James Watt invented the separate condenser for the steam engine.

1766 Oliver Goldsmith's *The Vicar of Wakefield* published.
Haydn's *Great Mass with Organ, in E flat* composed.
Henry Cavendish identified hydrogen and analysed air.

1768 James Cook's first voyage to the Antipodes.
Royal Academy of Arts founded in London.

1769 Sir Richard Arkwright established water-powered spinning mill.
Nicholas Cugnot experimented with his steam carriage: forerunner of the motor car.

1770 Goethe began *Dr Faustus*.
Captain James Cook entered Botany Bay in Australia.

1771 John Hunter wrote *Treatise on the Natural History of the Human Teeth* which provided framework for dentistry.

1772 Joseph Priestley, clergyman and chemist, discovered hydrochloric acid and nitrous oxide (laughing gas).
Daniel Rutherford, Scottish physicist, discovered nitrogen.

1773 Goldsmith's *She Stoops to Conquer* produced.
Assay offices opened in Sheffield and Birmingham.
Cook crossed Antarctic Circle: first explorer to do so, and sighted islands named after him.
Samuel Crompton invented spinning mule.
Calico introduced into England from Calicut, India, where it was first made.

1774 Priestley discovered oxygen and ammonia gas.

1775 Sheridan's *The Rivals* produced.
Beaumarchais' *Le Barbier de Séville* (Figaro), produced: plot for operas by Rossini and Mozart.
Mozart composed five violin concertos.

1776 Watt and Boulton in Birmingham factory constructed first practical steam engine.
Adam Smith wrote *Wealth of Nations*, famous economic work.
Edward Gibbon's *Decline and Fall of the Roman Empire* begun.

1777 John Howard, British prison reformer, published his treatise *The State of the Prisons*.
Lavoisier proved that air consisted of oxygen and nitrogen.

1778 Sheridan's *The School for Scandal* produced.
Thomas Coke of Holkham carried out experiments in cattle breeding, growing root crops to feed livestock, and the rotation of crops.
Joseph Bramah, British inventor, patented mechanism of water-closet.

1779 Abraham Darby built the first iron bridge in the world: in Shropshire.

1780 Robert Raikes, a publisher, opened his first Sunday School: in Gloucester.

1781 Rousseau's frank autobiography, *Confessions*, published.
Johann Pestalozzi's *Lienhard und Gertrud* published: new thoughts on the education of children.
Sir William Herschel discovered Uranus, the planet, and contributed pioneering ideas of the stellar system's structure.
Kant's *Critique of Pure Reason* laid foundation of modern philosophy.

1783 Mongolfier brothers made first successful ascent in fire balloon.

1784 Joseph Bramah patented safety lock.
Henry Cort, British ironmaster, took out his patent for dry-puddling pig iron to obtain wrought iron.
Pierre Laplace, French mathematician, wrote the first of his four great books.

1785 Edmund Cartwright invented power-loom.
First life-boat built by Lionel Lukin.
Solsano invented seismograph to measure earthquakes.
Withering used digitalis extracted from foxgloves to treat heart disease.

1786 Robert Burns wrote *Poems chiefly in the Scottish Dialect*.
Mozart's *The Marriage of Figaro* produced in Vienna.

1788 George Hepplewhite published book on furniture design.

1789 William Blake's *Songs of Innocence* published.
Gilbert White, Hampshire naturalist, wrote *Natural History of Selborne*.
Herschel used 40-foot telescope to discover two of Saturn's moons.
Lavoisier's *Elements of Chemistry*, which laid the foundation for modern chemistry, published.
France investigated conversion to metric system of measurement.

1791 Thomas Paine, philosopher, published *Rights of Man*.
James Boswell published his great biography *The Life of Samuel Johnson*.
Mozart composed *Die Zauberflöte (The Magic Flute)*; and wrote *Requiem* on his deathbed.
Wilberforce's *Motion for Abolition of Slave Trade* carried in Parliament.

1794 Haydn composed *Symphony in D (The Clock)* and *Symphony in G (The Military)*.
Eli Whitney invented cotton-gin for extracting cotton seed.

1795 Robert Southey's poems published.
François Appert invented preserving jar for keeping foods.
Joseph Bramah invented the hydraulic press.

1796 Edward Jenner carried out vaccination for smallpox.

1797 Nicolas Vauquelin, French chemist, discovered chromium.
John MacArthur laid foundation for wool industry in Australia.

1798 Wordsworth and Coleridge produced *Lyrical Ballads*, which included *Rime of the Ancient Mariner* and other famous poems.
Thomas Malthus wrote *Principle of Population*.
Hansard's Parliamentary Reports began.
Joseph Lancaster opened the first elementary school: in London.
Senefelder, German playwright, invented process of lithography in printing.

1800 Volta, Italian physicist, made first battery: of zinc and copper plates.

1801 Achard opened first sugar-beet factory.
Richard Trevithick invented steam road-carriage.

1803 John Dalton proposed an atomic theory of matter.
Trevithick built first successful railway locomotive.

1806 Sir Francis Beaufort introduced his scale of numbers to register wind strength: Beaufort Scale.

1808 Humphry Davy isolated barium, calcium, magnesium and strontium.
Gay-Lussac formulated Law of Volume of Gases.

1809 Beethoven composed the *Emperor Concerto*.

1810 Dalton explained atomic theory in *New System of Chemical Philosophy*: also produced carbon electric arc.
Macadam constructed roads.

1811 Krupp's iron works founded at Essen.

1812 Byron published *Childe Harold's Pilgrimage*.
Grimm's fairy tales published.
Henry Bell constructed steamship *Comet* to operate on the Clyde.

1813 Jane Austen's *Pride and Prejudice* published.

1814 Sir Walter Scott published *Waverley*.

1816 Sir David Brewster invented kaleidoscope.
René Laënnac invented stethoscope.

1817 John Constable painted *Flatford Mill*.
Baron Cuvier published *Animal Kingdom* and founded comparative anatomy and palaeontology.

1821 Michael Faraday expounded principle of electric motor.
Gay-Lussac and Arago made electro-magnet.
Charles Mackintosh invented process for rubberized waterproofing.

1825 George Stephenson constructed *The Rocket*, famous locomotive. His railway, Stockton to Darlington, opened: first passenger railway.
Faraday discovered benzene.

1826 Georg Ohm, German physicist, discovered mathematical law of electric currents (Ohm's Law).

1829 Louis Braille completed his system of finger-reading for the blind.
Joseph Henry constructed an electro-magnetic motor.
The Rocket won Rainham Trials and opened up the Railway Age.

1830 Alfred, Lord Tennyson's *Poems* published.
Alfred de Musset's French poems published.

1831 Balzac, Hugo, Stendhal published novels in France.
Faraday found means of producing electric current: leading to dynamo.

1833 Wheatstone Bridge invented for measuring electrical resistance.
Wheatstone invented the stereoscope.

1834 Faraday expounded laws of analysis.
Joseph Hansom patented the 'hansom cab'.
Cyrus H. McCormick patented the harvesting machine.

1835 Robert Browning wrote dramatic poem *Paracelsus*.
John Clare's *Rural Muse* published.
Donizetti's opera *Lucia di Lammermoor* produced.
Samuel Colt patented revolver.
Charles Darwin studied Galapagos Islands.
Faraday discovered self-induction of a coil of wire.

1836 Gogol wrote *The Inspector General*.

1837 Carlyle's *The French Revolution* published.
Charles Dickens wrote *Pickwick Papers* and *Oliver Twist*.
Pitman introduced his system of shorthand.
Wheatstone and Cooke invented first railway telegraph.
Samuel Morse invented system of telegraphy.

Index

The dates of all English monarchs are the dates of their reigns